Not So Easy Going

Not So Easy Going
The Policy Environments of Small Urban Schools and Schools-within-Schools

by

Mary Anne Raywid

and

Gil Schmerler

with

Stephen E. Phillips and Gregory A. Smith

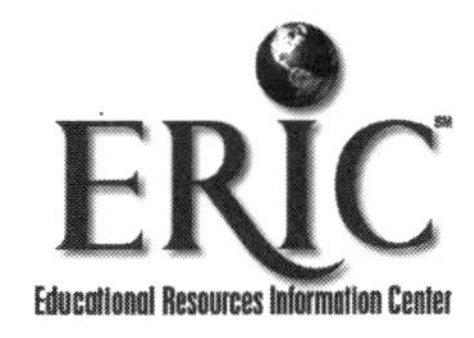

ERIC Clearinghouse on Rural Education and Small Schools
Charleston, WV

ERIC Clearinghouse on Rural Education and Small Schools

P.O. Box 1348
Charleston, WV 25325-1348
www.ael.org/eric/

Printed in the United States of America

Library of Congress Cataloging-in-Publication Data

Raywid, Mary Anne.
Not so easy going : the policy environments of small urban schools and schools-within-schools / Mary Anne Raywid and Gil Schmerler.
p. cm.
Includes bibliographical references and index.
ISBN 1-880785-26-9 (pbk. : alk. paper)
1. Urban schools—United States—Case studies. 2. Small schools—United States—Case studies. 3. School improvement programs—United States—Case studies. I. Schmerler, Gil. II. Title.
LC5131.R39 2003
371.2'5—dc21

ISBN 1-880785-26-9

Cover art by Michael Switzer, Design Works, Charleston, WV

An adapted version of chapter 1 appeared in the February 2002 issue of *Education Leadership.*

∞ The paper used in this publication meets the minimum requirements of the American National Standard for Information Sciences–Permanence of Paper for Printed Library Materials, ANSI Z39.481984.

The ERIC Clearinghouse on Rural Education and Small Schools is operated by AEL and funded by the U.S. Department of Education. AEL is a catalyst for schools and communities to build lifelong learning systems that harness resources, research, and practical wisdom. Information about AEL projects, programs, and services is available on our Web site or by writing or calling us. AEL is an affirmative action/equal opportunity employer.

This publication was prepared with funding from the Institute of Education Sciences (IES), U.S. Department of Education, under contract no. ED-99-CO-0027. The opinions expressed herein do not necessarily reflect the positions or policies of IES, the Department, or AEL.

Contents

Preface

The story of the effort to downsize our schools—to create small schools and schools-within-schools and small learning communities—is remarkable. In approximately the last dozen years, this idea has become one of the most favored of school reform strategies. One of the reasons is that during this period, quite a research record has been amassed to suggest the sorts of difference size makes. In fact, it has been established with a clarity and at a level of confidence that are rare in the annals of educational research.

We know that a great many youngsters learn more and better in small schools than in large ones, and that this is particularly true for disadvantaged or "at-risk" students.[1] Smaller schools and districts have been found, in multiple replications, to improve the odds of success for poor students, by halving the well-known negative effects of poverty on academic success.[2]

But smaller schools extend advantages to more fortunate youngsters as well: Kathleen Cotton reported that "a large body of research in the affective and social realms overwhelmingly affirms the superiority of small schools."[3] A collection of findings may have led her and others to this conclusion; for example, we know that proportionately far more students participate in cocurricular activities in smaller schools.[4] We know that there is less violence and vandalism in small schools and, in fact, that youngsters generally behave better in such surroundings.[5] We know that fewer students drop out of smaller schools.[6] More startlingly, it appears that small schools are less costly

---

[1]See Lee and Smith, "Effects of High School Restructuring and Size on Early Gains in Achievement and Engagement"; and Lee and Loeb, "School Size in Chicago Elementary Schools: Effects on Teachers' Attitudes and Students' Achievement."

[2]See Howley and Bickel, "The Influence of Scale."

[3]In Cotton, *Affective and Social Benefits of Small-Scale Schooling,* 1.

[4]See Pittman and Haughwout, "Influence of High School Size on Dropout Rate."

[5]See Stockard and Mayberry, *Effective Educational Environments.*

[6]See Fetler, "School Dropout Rates, Academic Performance, Size, and Poverty: Correlates of Educational Reform."

than large ones if assessed as to "expenditure per graduate" instead of "costs per pupil enrolled."[7]

We also know that teachers find working in small schools extremely rewarding. Their ability to make a difference in the lives of children—academically and beyond—is substantially increased; and the sense of efficacy that results makes a major difference.[8] In addition, teachers in small schools are likely to develop a greater awareness of, and fulfillment of, their own professionalism. In many small schools and schools-within-schools, their autonomy is expanded, and the programs they operate are programs they have chosen and designed. Finally, teachers in small schools are more dependent upon one another than those in large, bureaucratic schools, and this makes for extensive collaboration among the faculty, rather than the isolation in which teachers have long worked. The resulting help and support makes for a very different work scene. Even though they may work harder, small school teachers are more satisfied with their work, and morale is typically far higher than in conventional schools. As one Philadelphia teacher summed it up, despite bags under her eyes, "I've a smile on my face."

It follows that schools where students participate more, attend more regularly, are better behaved, and are less inclined to drop out, and where teachers are more committed and obtain more help from colleagues, are schools far different from those many of us know. They are transformed; that is, they are far more productive and all of their constituents are far more satisfied.

In general, the findings regarding the social and affective benefits of small schools have not involved the large number of cases standing behind the claims as to academic benefits. The same can be said about the claims regarding the benefits of the teacher collegiality small schools often stimulate. Nevertheless, the evidence on both these counts is sufficiently broad and extensive that it cannot be lightly dismissed.

Early in the twenty-first century, it would appear, then, that small schools have a lot going for them. The research demonstrating

[7]See Stiefel, Latarola, Fruchter, and Berne, *The Effects of Size of Student Body on School Costs and Performance in New York City High Schools.*

[8]See Bredeson, Fruth, and Kasten, "Organizational Incentives and Secondary School Teaching"; and Wasley et al., *Small Schools: Great Strides.*

superior results is increasingly conclusive and is reaching a broadening public. There are now several generations of small school graduates who can attest to the effectiveness of schools where they were known, valued, and respected. Thus, major foundations have targeted smaller schools for an unprecedented infusion of money. The federal government and many states, as well as dozens of large municipalities, have declared their core support for the development of "small learning communities."

Meanwhile, large schools, particularly in the cities, have proven highly resistant to meaningful reform and are often the breeding grounds of failure. Many youngsters are left to struggle under conditions that we know are highly likely to lead them to nothing but failure. And even with the aforementioned successes, the effort to create and sustain small schools, which has for the last several decades been bedeviled by bureaucratic resistance, public misunderstanding, and a mighty struggle for resources and autonomy, does not get much easier. Prodigious effort and brilliant maneuvering have enabled hundreds—possibly thousands—of small schools to navigate the rough waters of American school systems. But many have ultimately floundered, finding their energies depleted by policy and organizational environments that are inhospitable at best. And others are never attempted, as conscientious educators, who would certainly prefer to personalize and diversify schools, are frustrated early by the obstacles placed in their way.

The movement to create (and sustain existing) small schools will most certainly continue, however, because it is so profoundly necessary to so many parents, educators, and communities. And it will continue with increased urgency. But what can be done to ease the way for the next wave? How can we forestall the terrible waste of energy and talent that has typified this struggle? What can we learn from those who have succeeded in starting flourishing small schools and systems of small schools—and from those who have failed? What systems can be put in place, what policies adopted, what protections afforded that will help smooth the way for the schools to come? In short, how can we create policy environments that will ensure the existence of small schools for the students who so desperately need them?

This book is an attempt to look clearly and honestly at the often hostile environments in which small schools have had to try to make a go of it. By telling their stories, we attempt to identify the obstacles they face, spot potential flaws in certain strategies, and describe the systemic dysfunction that makes even good-faith efforts so difficult.

The picture is not a pretty one. This makes it all the more impressive that so many small schools have emerged from the bleakness with vitality and esprit and with enviable success records, and that so many dedicated educators continue to step forward to take up the challenge. For them—and for all who care about the future of public education—it is important to face and surmount the current organizational and bureaucratic realities. But envisioning changed policy environments that encourage, support, and sustain small schools will take more than wishful thinking. It will take candor, clarity, and endurance. We have tried here to show just what needs fixing.

What we aim to do is point out the *political* difficulties that small schools and schools-within-schools encounter with regulations, bureaucracies, and unions. We do not discuss the challenges they face in designing their programs or dealing with their students. There are other works that do that.[9] But these schools represent new kinds of organizations, and we focus on what they encounter in the bureaucratic systems within which they are situated. Our hope is to issue some warnings and to illustrate some of the changes that are needed in school systems to accommodate these new kinds of schools, or, for that matter, any new kind of school.

We Americans are caught in a dilemma: On the one hand, we know school reform is necessary if today's schools are going to work for today's school population, and thus we seek reform. Small schools, therefore, are intended to do more than just replicate the status quo on a smaller scale. The successful ones involve changes in curricular organization, instructional strategy, the organization of teachers' work, school culture, school and student assessment, and more. But an unresolved dilemma emerges: The people who undertake such changes by launching smaller schools find that these schools no longer fit in the very systems that were calling upon them to reform!

[9]See, for example, Raywid, *Focus Schools: A Genre to Consider* and *Taking Stock: The Movement to Create Mini-Schools, Schools-within-Schools, and Separate Small Schools.*

Several more things need be said in explaining what readers will find and not find in succeeding pages. First, we must underscore that we are not discussing rural schools. Our observations and experience are limited to small schools and schools-within-schools located mostly in large cities. We have included one chapter on a smaller city and one on an elementary school in a relatively small town, but no rural schools. We recognize that the situation of such schools may be quite different from what we point out. Suburban school downsizing efforts might well have been grist for our mill, but none are included here because we have not encountered them. It appears that with the small schools movement, the cities have clearly assumed the innovative leadership suburban schools once enjoyed.

In this book, then, we look first at districts and then at some individual schools. We were anxious to tell the stories of the three cities that have been most prominent in the movement to downsize schools—New York, Chicago, and Philadelphia—and we added Boston because of the uniqueness of its small schools and the special status they occupy. We have included two chapters on New York because we were able to obtain an account of the development of small schools there from the official whose office paved the way for them. Then, there are also accounts of individual small schools, and schools-within-schools, and a multiplex.[10]

The final point we want to make is that we are not attempting to provide full histories of the small schools in the places about which we write, or to bring readers up to date regarding the schools and districts we describe. Rather, we offer portions of their histories in order to present models or patterns of how schools-within-schools and small schools have begun and been installed in different places and the particular policy environments they experience. For instance, in Portland, we tell the story of how six teacher- and parent-launched *focus schools* got started and the problems they encountered. Today, a major district effort in Portland is espousing and supporting such programs. But we write only about particular focus schools and the problems they faced in an earlier period to illustrate the challenges confronting individual, grassroots-inspired programs.

---

[10]A multiplex is a school facility that houses two or more independent schools.

Each one of the patterns or models examined here comes with advantages and challenges of its own. We have studied and written about them in order to point out the pitfalls of starting small schools or schools-within-schools, and with the hope of eliminating these pitfalls, or, at minimum, helping people to be aware of them and to devise ways to circumvent them. We write with the hope of helping more people make small schools and schools-within-schools work because we believe that launching these schools is probably the best way yet devised to transform public education. The book ends with some conclusions we have reached about small school problems and possible solutions.

We want to thank the Joyce Foundation for making our observations and interviews in various locales possible. We also want to express our appreciation to all the people in all the locales who allowed themselves to be interviewed and to those who later helped check our manuscript for accuracy.

CHAPTER 1

Not So Easy Going

The pressures generating small schools have proved powerful over the last decade. They include the crisis in the cities, where substantial numbers of schools fail year after year. They also include the changing demographics of public education, with majorities in all cities—and foreseeably in a number of states—consisting of those populations considered to be most at risk of school failure. More recently, the pressures also include the threat of student violence—a terrifying issue in large schools but quite a negligible one in small schools.

As these pressures might suggest, those urging school downsizing are seeking a lot more than changes in school size. They also seek safer, more humane, and more effective schools that can reach an expanded variety of youngsters successfully. This calls for new school environments, programs, and organizational arrangements. Thus, the challenge of accommodating downsized units in educational organizations is more than simply making school smaller; it is a matter of accommodating new units that may look very different from the old ones and depart from them in fundamental ways.

Today, incentives are supplementing the pressures for school downsizing in quite influential ways. As of 2001, the federal government offered grants of up to $50,000 to large schools to convert to small learning communities. The Bill and Melinda Gates Foundation has committed a total of $250 million to generating small schools as a supplement to Ambassador Walter Annenberg's $500 million gift pledged almost a decade ago. A considerable portion of Annenberg's gift went to generating and sustaining small schools.

As a result of these pressures and incentives, districtwide initiatives to downsize large schools, a number of individual school initiatives (in St. Paul, Cincinnati, Seattle, and Sacramento), and some hybrid mixes of the two are springing up across the country. Indeed, we have created small schools and schools-within-schools (henceforth, *SWSs*) by the hundreds in the last 10 years.

Yet for many of them, the going has not been easy. One prominent reason is that we have yet to create the structures and policies necessary for them to thrive. We continue to bind these new organizational entities within old organizational structures, shackle them with outmoded practices, and restrict their success by imposing regulations designed for another time and place—while denying them the particular supports they need most.

Much has been written about the virtues and advantages of downsized schools, and some advice has been developed on how to bring about the transformation of the comprehensive high school or the oversized elementary school into *humanly* sized units. But very little has been written about what we need to do in order to permit small schools and SWSs to succeed. What kinds of conditions, controls, and supports external to these new units are essential to sustaining them?

The answers, we suspect, must be sought in two places: the organizational structures into which we place them and the policy environments with which we surround them. The two are not entirely separate, of course, but they can be made so. In the pages that follow, we shall see people addressing one or the other but rarely both. Sometimes, as we shall see, the best answer may appear to lie in structural change. Under other circumstances, the most viable solution to the same question may lie in policy change.

As different cities—New York, Philadelphia, and Chicago among them—and other locales have sought to downsize their schools, a number of patterns or models have been created for generating and fitting these new and small units into existing schools and districts. In the following pages we discuss the patterns we observed in the schools and districts we studied. Our list does not pretend to be exhaustive, but it does show the varied ways in which some schools and districts have responded to the school downsizing idea.

Pattern 1. Perhaps the oldest model is that of the large district creating a separate office with exclusive responsibility for the new units. This was the solution adopted in New York City in 1983 by then-Chancellor Tony Alvarado. The chancellor was seeking a way to encourage secondary school innovation, despite the policies of the city's High Schools Division—notoriously the educational bureaucracy's most rigid and intransigent office. Instead of trying to change the division, Alvarado created a new superintendency of alternative schools to launch innovative schools, represent them within the system, and oversee them with much more flexibility. The new office stood in the city's table of organization as the equal of the five borough high school superintendents, the only difference being that each borough superintendent controlled a contiguous area and the Office of Alternative Schools had schools and programs scattered throughout the five boroughs.

There were already almost 100 alternative schools and programs in the city, so the superintendent of alternative schools did not have to create all of them. As their numbers grew, some were organized by the superintendent, others by school principals, and yet others by self-selecting groups of teachers who approached the superintendent to authorize them as alternative schools. In the 1990s, when a number of new small high schools were launched, most asked to affiliate with the Office of Alternative Schools. As of 1997, the city's alternative schools numbered 425.[1]

The alternative schools office operated somewhat analogously to the way Alvarado himself had operated years earlier when he cultivated a famous set of elementary schools in one of New York's 32 community school districts. As superintendent of Community School District 4 in the 1970s, he had invited self-selecting groups of teachers to launch programs, which he placed in any school with the space to accommodate them. Although these were, in a physical sense, SWSs,

[1]New York has no definition of alternative schools, other than to say that students at such schools have been in trouble in their prior schools. The definition is loose enough so that it could include a large majority of the city's students.

they reported not to the principal but directly to the district superintendent's office, and Alvarado as district superintendent functioned as their protector. His associate superintendent was later placed in charge of the *alternative concept schools*, as they were called, and served in a capacity much like the alternative schools office Alvarado later established as chancellor of the city's schools.

The crux of this model is that self-selecting groups of teachers are invited to launch small schools or SWSs, and a high-ranking school official—the superintendent, or an associate superintendent—then directly oversees these units instead of having them report to principals or middle level central office managers. Moreover, unless the overseer is the superintendent, oversight of the new units is the sole function of the officer to whom they are assigned.

Pattern 2. A somewhat different model existed in Philadelphia between 1994 and 2000, when school downsizing was the centerpiece of the superintendent's program. Instead of turning to organizational structure to bring about downsizing, Superintendent David Hornbeck used policy. He launched *small learning communities* with the mandate that no unit in Philadelphia schools could exceed 400 students. Any school with an enrollment larger than 400 would have to break itself down into separate and distinct units. The units were then overseen by their building principals, who were responsible for carrying out the superintendent's mandate: downsize; create a distinctive theme for each unit; and, eventually, give students or families a choice among units.

Such an approach has both liabilities and assets. The strong point, of course, is the possibility of improving all schools from the start of the mandate. The weakness is that a mandated effort—and one of such scale—is likely to succeed slowly, if at all. Hornbeck, however, had clear and plausible plans for helping schools move from shaky starts to successful development.

Pattern 3. Boston represents still another pattern. The 11 well-known small schools there were intended from the start as innovative departures to be given broad freedom. Interestingly, the arrangement was initially proposed by the Boston Teachers Union. The union recommended the launching of "Pilot" schools to serve two purposes: to demonstrate the establishment's (i.e., the school system's and union's) ability to be creative and to permit innovation, and to provide an alternative to the charter schools being launched in Boston and elsewhere in Massachusetts. Both the union that proposed them, and the superintendent who supported the idea, hoped that the Pilot schools would become sources of ideas and inspiration throughout the city. There is a coordinator of Pilot schools in the central office, but he has not functioned as a strong advocate.

In a number of ways, the Pilots appear to be thriving, though many feel their independence from the system continues to be a constant struggle. Some in the central offices grouse that what these schools are doing is not being shared.[2]

Pattern 4. Chicago represents yet another model: small schools there have been formally blessed and encouraged by the school board but, until recently, they have had no strong champion at central headquarters. The district's table of organization designated the assistant to the associate superintendent for instruction as their liaison. This title was later changed to director of the Office of Special Initiatives, and the director oversaw small schools as well as an array of special projects. But the director was assigned no staff or budget. And while the authority and voice of small schools within the system has been notably weaker in Chicago than in the three cities described earlier, this has been offset somewhat by an unusually strong alliance with the business and professional, philanthropic, and academic communities. Recently, the staff counsel of one of the key organizations, the Business and Professional People for the Public Interest, became director of the system's new Office of Small Schools. The creation of this office, plus the support of the present CEO of Chicago's schools, augur well for the fortunes of small schools in that city.

Pattern 5. Yet another pattern consists of SWSs created at the individual school level, rather than at the district level, and at the instigation of the principal. (This contrasts with the Community School District 4 model described in Pattern 1, where the superintendent invited teacher groups to form and come to him with proposals; in this model, it is the principal who initiates the action.) The Kapaa

[2]The position of the schools is that they are willing to share but unwilling to organize occasions for doing so. This, they feel, is the district's responsibility.

Elementary School on Hawaii's island of Kauai represents this model. There, a new principal of an elementary school enrolling 1,500 students sought to reduce the oversized school to more humane dimensions by inviting and encouraging self-selecting groups of teachers to design their own separate school-within-a-school (SWAS). None were ordered to do so, but over a four- or five-year period, and with the proffering of incentives, the school was gradually converted into eight SWSs, each with its own teacher leader. Kauai's SWSs were afforded particularly strong support within the school but very little support from the system outside it.

Pattern 6. A final pattern, and probably the most prevalent one until quite recently, is the grassroots model in which a group of teachers, or a group of parents and teachers, decides to try to launch a SWAS, and seeks the principal's authorization for doing so. Each arrangement and prerogative must then be negotiated with the principal. Of the six patterns described here, this probably represents the weakest and most unstable, since the unit exists at the pleasure of the principal. Any change in that office can terminate it. This is the position of the six SWSs, called *focus schools*, in Portland, Oregon. They are currently seeking a firmer and more favorable footing within that district.

As the six different organizational patterns reflected in our list suggest, there are many ways to insert small schools and SWSs into a school district's table of organization or that of a single school. A superintendent can go a long way toward creating nurturant conditions by exercising the option of altering the table of organization, as was done in the creation of the Office of Alternative Schools in New York. But SWSs can sometimes survive comfortably with only the principal's support. With neither, it may be rough going despite rhetoric from the top about the virtues of smallness, or resolutions in favor of downsizing.

The source of the policy environments surrounding small schools and SWSs can differ considerably. For the small school, policies emanating from the district level are usually important. Yet, standing rules, regulations, and procedures written for quite different types of institutions do not always fit small and different sorts of schools, and so these schools pose a real challenge to school districts. As Judith Rizzo, deputy chancellor of New York City Schools, put it:

> We are convinced that small schools cannot flourish on the margins of the system; they need to be an integral part of it. Nor can the system flourish if it can accommodate only one organizational model, if it discourages change, or if it inhibits innovation, whether by design or by a failure to adapt.[3]

Despite such a bold stance on the part of school districts in New York and elsewhere, the standard approach to dealing with difficulties imposed by rules that don't fit has been to exercise *policy by exception*, as noted several years ago by Linda Darling-Hammond and Jacqueline Ancess.[4] Instead of seeking new and different policies to govern the new schools, there has been a tendency simply to settle for waivers and exemptions to existing policy. This is highly injurious to small schools in a number of respects (see Chapter 11).

Turning now from the small school to SWSs, or to a single SWAS, the most immediate policy environment is typically created by the building principal. The first major policy difficulty with this arrangement stems from instability, since in many, if not most, locales, a principal supportive of the SWSs organizational structure is often replaced by one insufficiently supportive to permit it to do well, or even one sufficiently hostile to terminate the arrangement.

The second major policy difficulty faced by SWSs stems from control issues. Principals are accustomed to being the center of authority, decision making, and monitoring within their schools. The SWSs structure challenges such centralized control. It invites diversity, rendering control and oversight of the resulting differentiated units more difficult and awkward to sustain. (A set of SWSs that are essentially identical to one another in school climate, curricular organization, pedagogy, and approach defeats the ultimate purpose of school downsizing, and that is to cultivate schools that can succeed with an increasingly broad range of youngsters. It also defeats the proximate purpose of generating among students a strong sense of affiliation with their SWAS.)

The third major source of policy difficulties among SWSs centers on the principal's sense of responsibility for keeping the school a

---

[3]In Rizzo, "School Reform: A System Approach," 148.

[4]See Darling-Hammond et al., "Inching toward Reform in New York City."

cohesive unit. The Effective Schools movement of the 1970s and 1980s emphasized the principal's responsibility to nurture a sense of unified purpose or mission throughout the entire school. In the playing out of daily school life, this premise can conflict intensely with the notion of separate and distinctive SWSs. Some schools, for instance, have had difficulty over matters such as one behavior and discipline code versus several; one graduation ceremony versus several; and which takes precedence, the demands of orchestra and athletic teams or the SWAS schedule.

In high schools, there is often a fourth major source of policy-related difficulty that stems from the role and prerogatives of department chairs. The SWAS structure is not simply a departure from or modification of the traditional high school structure, which is horizontally divided into subject areas. SWSs recommend a vertical structure instead, organizing teachers of diverse subjects and grade levels into a unit. Thus, in those high schools that simply add SWSs while retaining department chairs and their prerogatives, an ongoing tension should be expected between the "old order" and the new. When department chairs call meetings, for example, they can create conflicts with teachers' obligations to and within the new units. The challenge exists in somewhat weaker form in larger elementary schools, where the SWSs organization replaces the grade-level organization that is sometimes prominent and powerful. Grade-level organization, however, is rarely as strong at the elementary level as departmental organization is in the high school, which may well be why elementary schools are notoriously easier to change than secondary schools.

This, then, is a brief introductory overview of the types and sources of policy-related challenges often faced by SWSs. The policy environments of small schools—as distinct from SWSs—are somewhat different. They are, in the first place, more remote and less immediate. But they can be as constricting. For instance, one New York City regulation required all city high schools to schedule their students by computer, negating the individualization that many small schools see as their central raison d'etre! Yet, it proved impossible to convince those monitoring the scheduling process to exempt anyone from it. This provoked all sorts of evasive and extra-legal tactics among faculties sufficiently committed to their mission of tailoring educational programs to individuals. In another case, the small-school practice of placing students in volunteer positions in the community for half a day each week—in the dual interests of making the benefits of service learning available to them and of providing extended teacher interaction time—was cancelled by a district policy requiring all students to be in classrooms for five full days each week.

As these examples suggest, one of the major difficulties the policy environment sometimes imposes on small schools is barring what the schools see as important—even central—to their mission, or mandating what is anathema. In fact, to the extent that the small schools do actually represent new and innovative institutions, this is quite likely to happen. Such seems to be the case with the tests now being imposed by the accountability and standards movements. Many of the more creative schools have rigorous and carefully devised performance standards their students must meet as an alternative to testing. In a number of these institutions, alternative forms of assessing the acquisition of skills and the mastery of knowledge is a major part of their innovation and integral to their design. In those states where standards have become tantamount to standardization when it comes to assessment, it may prove increasingly difficult to sustain much curricular or even pedagogical innovation of any sort.

CHAPTER 2

Birthing the Small Schools Movement: New York

The small schools idea was launched in New York City 30 years ago. It began in Community School District 4 in 1973, when the new young superintendent of the Spanish Harlem district knew he had to do something drastic to improve education there. At the time, District 4 ranked 32nd of the city's 32 districts on virtually any quality or effectiveness indicator. So, the superintendent invited his teachers to collect a few colleagues and design their own program. He also invited at least one teacher from outside the district to do so. She was Deborah Meier, and when she became convinced that Superintendent Anthony Alvarado really meant what he said—that he would find them their own separate space, relax regulations for them, and buffer them from outside interference—she accepted.

Although District 4 teachers were at first very wary and hesitant about accepting the superintendent's invitation, over the next 15 years, 26 groups did so and opened what were, in effect, their own small schools. All of them were placed in existing school buildings, but with the superintendent's protection. Thus, in effect, they were not under the principal's supervision but the superintendent's. Eventually, as the number of schools grew larger, Alvarado named his associate superintendent director of alternative concept schools.

From the start, the district had atypical freedom from the controls exerted by the city's central education bureaucracy. Several reasons for this have been offered. One is that officials had, in effect, written off District 4 as hopeless anyway, so there was no point in trying to monitor it; hence, they just weren't looking and didn't know about the changes that were under way there. Another explanation is that city education officials felt the district's schools were so bad that anything, including rule departures, might be an improvement. A third reason for District 4's relative freedom from bureaucratic constraints is that it openly practiced and recommended "creative noncompliance." Actually, the term is a bit of a misnomer because what the district was doing was attempting to comply with the letter of the law while evading, or end running, its intent, in the interests of better serving children. For instance, Alvarado remained in compliance with a regulation on requirements for occupants of particular positions by simply "vacating" the positions. He didn't violate the requirements for occupants but simply abolished the positions.

Clearly, teachers who launched these small, or alternative concept, schools enjoyed an extraordinarily positive policy environment. As suggested above, there was little interference from city officials. Within the district, their schools were the superintendent's project and he went out of his way to protect them. If they encountered difficulties posed by building principals, he intervened on their behalf. They were also given a great deal of support in the form of grant monies, which the district began to seek and obtain. Those who were involved look back on this period as halcyon days.

In light of his success, which gradually came to be known across the city, Alvarado was invited in 1983 to become Chancellor of New York City Schools. His successor superintendent in District 4, Carlos Medina, had been a part of the alternative concept schools team and sustained them enthusiastically. Meanwhile, Alvarado sought to accomplish at the central office level changes comparable to those he had introduced at the district level. But there was much more resistance to be overcome in the large bureaucracy. His major solution was to create the alternative schools superintendency to encourage and nourish innovative schools. Stephen Phillips, whom he named superintendent, tried to operate in relation to his schools as Alvarado had operated in relation to the alternative concept schools of District 4. But the challenges he encountered were far different from the relatively minor obstacles Alvarado had encountered in his comparatively isolated district 10 years earlier, and they called for different solutions. The story of the alternative schools superintendency, and that of its superintendent for the first 14 years, is told in chapter 3.

Meanwhile, in the mid-'80s, District 4 opened two high schools: the Manhattan Center for Science and Mathematics and Central Park East Secondary School. This was somewhat extraordinary, since in New York, elementary and middle schools are operated by the 32 community school districts, but high schools are run by an entirely different authority: the citywide High Schools Division. (A relative few are supervised by the Office of Alternative Schools.) Both of these new District 4 high schools opted, however, to become affiliated with the Office of Alternative Schools instead of the far more tightly controlling High Schools Division. In fact, since both enrolled 7th to 12th graders, involving both the district's middle school bailiwick and the high schools' bailiwick, both schools came under the supervision of two authorities: the district and the Office of Alternative Schools.

Had it been two other offices, their path could have been quite difficult. However, given the orientation of these two, both tried to smooth the way. This was not the case with the small schools opened in the '90s. Most of these schools sought affiliation with the Office of Alternative Schools, but many were simply assigned to the High Schools Division. These schools had to serve two masters—the district superintendent and the borough superintendent representing the High Schools Division. With two different sets of expectations, two different cultures, and two different sets of regulations and procedures, life was often hard.

Unfortunately, Alvarado did not remain long as chancellor, and his hopes for expanding innovation throughout the city's schools left with him. But, in 1990, after several intervening chancellors, Joe Fernandez was appointed to the post. His superintendency in Dade County, Florida, immediately prior to this provided strong evidence of his commitment to teacher empowerment. His tenure as New York City Schools chancellor is remembered particularly for two things: the school-based management and shared decision-making plan he attempted to launch, and the more successful small schools movement he got under way.

Beginning in the early '90s, teachers and others were invited to submit proposals for small schools. Some were launched by the city; some were virtually designed by outside groups, such as unions and civic organizations; some were conceived by the Center for Collaborative Education (the New York arm of the Coalition for Essential Schools); and some were sponsored by the New Visions project of the Fund for New York City Public Education.

The venture involving the Center for Collaborative Education (CCE) got under way in 1992 with the help of local foundation funds. It was intended to solve the problem of the city's failing high schools by replacing them with "smaller, more intimate and academically intensive learning environments."[1] The venture, named the Coalition Campus Project, was also intended as a model for starting new schools. It involved an existing school (a CCE member) providing considerable assistance to a like-minded, prospective principal or director for a new school. CCE helped this leader design the new school, select its teachers, find space, and get ready for start-up, all over the period of a year. Once under way, the CCE mentor school (a designation that was actually rejected due to its status-differential connotations) continued to provide help and advice as sought. And, since the new schools became members of the CCE, help was available from a number of like-minded people embarked on similar ventures. Altogether, the Coalition Campus Project launched 11 new schools.

The Fund for Public Education in New York represented a number of philanthropies and channeled funds into the schools. With the blessings of Chancellor Fernandez, its New Visions Project, established in 1992, issued a request for proposals with the promise of launching 25 new small schools. Unlike CCE, New Visions was not trying to expand the number of schools of a particular type. They were willing to, and did, fund progressive schools and quite conservative ones as well. After a careful screening and selection process, New Visions funded 15 new small schools. It later sponsored a second-round request for proposals which, combined with the first round, resulted in a total of 29 schools.

---

[1]In Darling-Hammond et al., "Reinventing High School," 1 (of original manuscript).

Meanwhile, in 1993, an Annenberg Challenge grant had come to New York. Its stated goals were "to increase the number of small, excellent schools of choice in New York City, to change the educational system so that it better supports and maintains such schools, and to effect systemwide public school reform."[2] Not surprisingly, the first of these goals proved far easier to achieve than the last two.

Of the Annenberg Challenge grant funds to New York, most were spent on helping new schools already launched and establishing four networks of support for these schools. The four were the Center for Collaborative Education, which, as mentioned earlier, had established the Coalition Campus Project and created 11 new schools; New Visions, which had established 29 new schools; the Center for Educational Innovation of the Manhattan Institute, which had helped establish a number of new schools in New York and elsewhere (e.g., in Community School District 3, they helped develop diversified schools of choice throughout the district); and ACORN, an organization that had worked largely on housing issues for low-income minority groups but had also sponsored one new small high school, a New Visions school. Of the four networks, two—CCE and ACORN—were committed to schools of particular orientations and approaches. The other two were not, and were glad to lend support to promising proposals recommending a variety of orientations. The result of such a broad receptivity range, however, was that two of the networks had the capacity to foster close relationships and extensive interaction and support among their members, while the other two did not.

There seems to have been only one head-on effort on the part of New York's Annenberg networks to change the educational system—the second purpose announced for the grant. This was an interesting school governance proposal worked out by Deborah Meier to substitute *Learning Zones* for the city's districts and hierarchies. Her idea was that each school would become connected with other schools of the same bent (orientation, focus, philosophy), irrespective of their location within the city, and the group would hold all member schools accountable to meeting professional standards. Noncontiguous zones would, in effect, replace districts, and interactive professional monitoring would replace bureaucratic school control.

---

[2]In Domanico, "A Small Footprint on the Nation's Largest School System," 9.

As adapted and set forth to city education officials by the networks, the idea was to create a single Learning Zone, including all of the Annenberg schools, which would be organized into four networks for governance purposes. As Ray Domanico points out in his appraisal of the Annenberg grant in New York (2000)—and as many of those involved still remember it—there was not much agreement among the networks on this Learning Zone proposal. CCE saw it as the systemic reform route promised in the Annenberg grant proposal they had submitted. The Center for Educational Innovation, however, was less interested in system reform. As analyst Domanico put it,

> They had little interest in altering the structure of the district system, as their strongest working relationships were with local superintendents. They believed in working through the existing structure and saw efforts to undermine it as counter-productive and futile. And under such conditions, the learning zone idea, that would have been extremely difficult to sell to a bureaucracy anyway, simply went nowhere.[3]

In less than two years, Chancellor Cortines, who succeeded Fernandez, following an interim and acting superintendent, was replaced by Rudy Crew. The small schools had managed to survive following the departure of Chancellor Fernandez, who espoused them. They had survived through an interim and acting chancellor, and then through Cortines, who seemed to accept them but without much discernible conviction that they were the solution to the city's school ills. Now, things became much harder under Chancellor Crew.

Crew was a recentralizer. He managed to convince the state legislature, in effect, to rescind the authority granted the 32 districts under the decentralization legislation of 1968. With the new law, he obtained the right to override (1) the election of local district board members, (2) their choice of a district superintendent, and (3) that individual's choice of particular principals. As the law put it, Crew had the right to remove any of these officials.

Now, obviously, this augured poorly for the autonomy sought and needed by the new schools. One ominous step was the abrupt replacement, in 1997, of Stephen Phillips as superintendent of alterna-

[3]Ibid., 10.

tive schools, a post he had held since Alvarado appointed him 14 years earlier. Another was the decision that any new small schools launched by any authority—the districts, the CCE, or New Visions, all of which had been authorized to establish them—would first have to obtain the OK of the chancellor's office. And when a school established by New Visions was failing badly enough that the sponsor asked the new superintendent of alternative schools to close it down, he refused to do so and simply assigned the principal of a large failing high school to take it over. There was also a move to set minimum enrollments for small schools at 400, 600, and 800 respectively for elementary, middle, and high schools. And although the chancellor backed off on the minima after a groundswell of objections, indicating instead that decisions would be made on a case-by-case basis, individual small schools were pressured by the new alternative schools superintendent to increase their enrollments by 100 students.

Chancellor Crew made it explicit that although "he supported the concept of small schools . . . they were not central to his mission of rebuilding the system." The major reason, explained the chancellor was "the question of scalability. And the only things we want to bring to scale are those things which can . . . be replicated. . . ."[4] This was a direct blow, since small schools seek to replace the impersonality of rule-driven institutions with personal interactions; the latter are always person-driven and hence not replicable as a model to be set in operation anywhere.

Another blow came from the administrators union, the Council of Supervisors and Administrators (CSA), which managed to obtain an arbitrator's ruling that the small schools would have to have principals, not just teacher directors. Since a sizeable majority of the small schools had teacher directors as a matter of principle and preference, as well as for reasons of economy, this was a severe blow. In a single stroke, it put firm limits on innovation with respect to school organization, and it raised the costs of operating small schools.

The teachers union, in contrast to the CSA, had supported small schools. The United Federation of Teachers had been willing to waive teacher assignment and seniority transfer rights, recognizing that the integrity of these schools depended on having like-minded teachers

---

[4]In Hartocollis, "Small Schools Face Limits on Autonomy," B1.

who shared the vision of their colleagues. Thus, the union accepted teacher selection by a school personnel committee consisting mainly of teachers. In fact, with the approval of district officials, the union even helped prepare CCE members to participate in selecting teachers for the new schools. Perhaps the largest single systemic reform associated with the small schools to date emerged from this experience. A "School-Based Option" provision became part of the teachers' union contract with the city. Upon the vote of 75 percent of a school's teachers, the selection of new teachers is handled by a teacher personnel committee. Such a vote also frees the school from seniority transfer provisions that enable the replacement of teachers during the school year by others with more seniority.

The small schools continued to be shackled by regulations, though, some of which made good sense in principle but simply did not fit. For example, as told in chapter 8, New York has a rule to the effect that in all schools of choice, admissions should represent a spread of achievement levels, with no more than 16 percent of those admitted scoring above average in reading, no more than 16 percent scoring below, and the rest scoring in the middle range. Some such regulation makes sense in order to prevent selective and elitist schools. But it was unreasonable to apply such a rule to schools designed explicitly for at-risk students, who were likely to cluster at the bottom of the city's score distributions. It was particularly inappropriate to apply it to International High School, which had a program designed specifically for students who could not speak, much less read, English. Yet the city tried to insist that International have the same reading achievement distributions required of all city schools! It has taken a great deal of evasion and subterfuge—and hence time and effort—to end run this regulation.

In the early '90s, when a number of small schools were getting started, many of them could not meet the city's schedule for student assignments. Choices and assignments throughout the city were completed before the newcomers could begin their enrollment process. Thus, they were left with a pool of youngsters who had not been admitted or had not applied to other schools. This left some of the new schools with a larger group of at-risk and more challenging students than most schools.

Space proved extremely difficult to find in a city with a growing school population, and little help was extended by city officials. As a result, some of the new schools had to begin in one set of quarters and move to another during the first school year. As reported in a detailed history of the Coalition Campus Project (CCP) schools,[5] two of these schools had to move as many as three times during their first year of operation! (Moving midyear from one area of the city to another was bad enough in a place like New York, which has good public transportation facilities. In places where this is not the case and midyear moves have been necessary, some students must enter a new school in midsemester, and the relocated school must recruit a new population.)

The story of the CCP schools, as told by Darling-Hammond, Ancess, and Ort[6] involves almost a circus of timing problems and delays on the part of city officials. The need for a number of ill-coordinated offices to approve things, and other snafus, led to costly delays on almost everything. Job postings had to be approved by the central office and their delays postponed by as long as six months the hiring of directors for the CCP schools. Teacher hiring was similarly delayed, and this cut severely into joint, preopening planning time, a central design feature of the schools. A new computer system prevented the hiring of secretaries until after school opened. Purchasing deadlines required the ordering of materials before staff had been hired and the designation of delivery sites before space had been acquired, leaving some schools without furniture when school opened.

As difficult as these start-up problems were (and there were others that continued at the hands of the city's central office), perhaps the greatest threat to the small schools came not from the city but the state. In that struggle, the city, in fact, became an ally. The issue was, and continues to be, the state testing program. New York State is known for the Regents Examinations it has administered for almost a century. But until five or six years ago, they were administered only to college bound high school students, and not even to all of those (since not all of the state's high schools, even in affluent districts, elected to give them). Thus, only a relatively small percentage of high school

---

[5]See Darling-Hammond et al., "Reinventing High School."

[6]Ibid.

students took these tests. Now, however, the New York State Commissioner of Education has decreed that all students in every New York high school must pass the Regents Exams in order to graduate.

This requirement has posed a severe threat to the new small schools, many of which attribute their success, in part, to the alternative ways in which they assess student accomplishment. In many, although the requirements of their assessments are high, they do not include standardized tests. Moreover, the requirement of the Regents Exams will also affect curriculum and the way it is organized and delivered. Many small-school proponents claim that the effectiveness of these schools is heavily attributable to their present curricular approaches and that to change them in order to accommodate the exams is to risk an impressive record of success. Seventy-one percent of a sample of students attending four of the new CCE schools graduated within four years, and of these, 89 percent went on to college. These schools reported no dropouts.[7]

When the commissioner first rejected requests from the small schools to accept alternative assessments in lieu of the Regents Exam for English, his decision vitalized a consortium of 40 of New York's small schools. The commissioner has since extended his ruling to require the exams in all subjects. The consortium has filed a class action suit to block the ruling. Whether it will prevail is yet to be seen. It remains a struggle between two forces: those who recognize that schools must improve but are reluctant to see them heading down new paths for doing so and those who are struggling—often with considerable effectiveness—to meet today's educational challenges in novel ways.

International High School is one of the small schools that, under duress, has managed to accommodate the Regents Exams while slightly relaxing its previous portfolio assessment requirements. And Eric Nadelstern, International's founding principal, is keeping the city's small schools movement very much alive. Nadelstern left International and moved to the Bronx, where he became New York's first deputy superintendent of New and Small Schools. His borough, where it appeared that every single high school would soon be on the

[7]See Ancess and Ort, *How the Coalition Campus Schools Have Reimagined High School.*

state's list of failing schools, was more than due for major change. When he put out a request for proposals for new small schools, there were 90 letters of intent from all over the city!

According to plan, in two years, he will have 15 new small high schools up and running in the Bronx. They will be housed in what are now six failing high schools. He also plans to try to model a way in which school systems can accommodate genuine reform without strangling it. Nadelstern's idea is to create within the area a "Zone of Innovation" that will oversee the new schools. The current supervisory fragmentation that typically marks bureaucracies involve a separate supervisor of each program and curricular area who oversees how his or her particular specialty is carried out within 20 schools. Nadelstern intends to replace this with a new set-up in which a single supervisor is totally responsible for perhaps four schools. The detailed knowledge of the schools being overseen that this arrangement will permit is, he feels, the analog to what the small schools have done in restructuring themselves.

Despite some failures, New York's small schools have been enormously successful. And while this success has sometimes been aided by top officials, it has always been furthered by the ability of school staff to deal effectively with, or somehow manage to end run, the middle management officials who comprise the bureaucracy.

Chapter 3

A Separate Superintendency

Stephen E. Phillips

As described in chapter 2, in New York City's decentralized school system, established by the state legislature in 1968, only the high schools remained centralized. They are governed by a single office, the High School Division. The division is represented in each of the city's five boroughs by a borough superintendent of high schools. In 1983, New York's then-chancellor, Anthony Alvarado, named an additional superintendent—a superintendent of alternative schools—to oversee alternative schools all over the city, scattered throughout the boroughs.

The broadly understood reason that Alvarado established the new superintendency was to improve secondary education, at least in some schools, by circumventing the High Schools Division. The division was widely held to be the single most difficult office in a bureaucracy known for its rigidity. Instead of trying to reform the division and its subposts throughout the city (the five boroughs), Alvarado sought instead to establish a new office that would encourage innovation among its schools and creativity among their teachers. More explicitly, Alvarado told me, as the first appointee to the post of superintendent of alternative schools, that he wanted the superintendency to accomplish three things. First, he wanted to create a "strength in numbers" effect among the alternative high schools and programs that already existed. Second, he was looking for a locus of advocacy for alternative education. And third, he wanted to see the number of alternative high schools and programs within the city expanded.

When the alternative schools office opened, the city's alternative schools only served the kids other schools had wanted to get rid of and youngsters who had dropped out of school. But that situation was certainly not what Alvarado wanted to proliferate. He had come to the chancellorship from Community School District 4 in Spanish Harlem, where, as the young superintendent responsible for launching schools that were attracting international attention, he had created a number of what he called *alternative concept schools.* These were unique institutions created by self-selecting groups of teachers with a shared conception of what an education should consist of and what a school should look like. In 1983, some of these District 4 schools were nearly a decade old and yielding unprecedented success among school populations most would have written off as destined for failure. This is the kind of operation Alvarado hoped to cultivate and nurture in establishing the alternative schools superintendency.

In 1983, when the office opened, there were 11 alternative high schools. Shortly thereafter, education programs in drug rehabilitation facilities and in a number of GED preparation sites (the Rikers Island prison, the School for Pregnant Girls, Auxiliary Services, and Outreach) were transferred to the new office. By the end of the 1983-84 school year, the alternative schools superintendency was responsible for 97 sites, serving 16,500 students.

Initially few, if any, of the these schools had been launched by school officials. Rather, they had been started by community-based organizations and activist groups with the aid of state or federal funding. When the Nixon administration ended that funding, these formerly independent schools reluctantly became part of the New York City school system in order to survive. In many, borough superintendents who sought to improve them by making them as much like other high schools as possible then stamped out the creative, innovative dimensions that had helped their programs succeed.

Prior to Alvarado's chancellorship, only one chancellor, Harvey Scribner, had shown much interest in fundamental reform. He sought to introduce some high schools with novel, less formal ways of "doing school." When the High Schools Division refused to cooperate, the chancellor's office itself sent out requests for proposals and hired the directors of several new schools, including City-As-School and Middle College High School, both of which have since been adopted and adapted in locations all over the country.[1] But the directors of the new programs were given a hard time by the High Schools Division, which did things like withholding funding, denying space, and refusing access to schools for purposes of recruiting students. One of the new school directors was told, for instance, that the only students he could recruit were those from the long-term absentee lists of two vocational schools.

As such a history suggests, the Office of Alternative Schools could not look to the High Schools Division, of which it was a part, for a great deal of help. Yet, over the 14-year period I directed that office, it managed to grow and thrive. By 1997, there were 59 schools and programs at 425 sites enrolling more than 47,500 students. Moreover, a number of these new schools and programs had been started precisely in the spirit of alternative concept schools, where the point was not doing the same thing at a different place but doing school quite differently from the traditional mold. The total when I left office included a large number of the schools launched in connection with the small schools movement that began in the early '90s.

How did it happen? How were the alternative schools in my jurisdiction allowed to operate their own programs relatively free of the overwhelming constraints imposed on the city's other high schools? I used to say, only partly in jest, that I spent more than half my time trying to figure out ways to end run the bureaucracy and its rules. But actually, there was a bit more to it than that. There were three fundamental ways in which I tried to operate, in order to get more alternative schools started, and then protect them and allow them to flourish. First, what was most evident and most overarching was an attempt to win and protect their freedom to carry out their own

[1]City-As-School is a school in which students' work consists extensively of observing and participating in city civic offices, cultural centers, and work places. Middle College High School is a program primarily directed at high-risk students. It is conducted on the campus of, and shares classes and activities with, a community college. Both of these schools still operate in New York.

programs. Second was an attempt to influence the implementation of state and local education policy in their interests. And third was an effort to seize upon and take maximum advantage of whatever opportunities came along that could aid in the creation and sustenance of innovative schools.

A number of my bureaucratic superordinates and fellow superintendents accused me of "giving away the store" in my relations with my schools, and I've also been accused of letting them get away with murder. But controlling them was not my intent. I wanted to see them accomplish first-rate results with youngsters lacking the middle class background and support upon which traditional schools consistently rely. I felt that the best chance for this to happen was through enabling my schools to develop their own visions and carry out their own plans for engaging their students. Thus, instead of encouraging subservience, I became impatient with those few alternative schools that constantly asked for direction and continued to assume that some approving officer had to validate every step before they took it.

Of course, some supervision was needed, particularly of new schools and programs, and they got it. There were also a few instances in which principals had to be replaced, and they were. But for me these were not the kinds of activities that defined the office. Within a year of assuming it, I was thinking in terms of what I called the "Service Superintendency." Here's how I tried to provide it.

First, I never built a large staff for the office. While other New York superintendencies of comparable enrollments had 20 to 30 professionals in their offices, the alternative schools office had only 9. To have more would necessitate that they all have something to do, and that would invite the mandating of more demands and structure in the schools, followed by the need for more oversight and supervision. So the office remained small.

A considerable amount of our time went into devising ways to avoid regulatory compliance by freshly and "creatively" interpreting regulations. For example, New York State has long held that high school students must have four years of social studies education. But it does not require that instruction to occur over four years or be spread over 40 weeks of five-day-a-week periods of 40 minutes each. And it does not say that there must be separate courses for global studies, American history, and civics. We found that by rearranging time and course design, we could meet the broad outlines of the requirements while doing things quite differently than the comprehensive high schools.

For instance, some small schools rotate their curriculum instead of rotating their students through a curriculum. One year, students in all grades, 9-12, take American History. The next year's offering is Non-Western Cultures, and all are enrolled. The following year, students take Western Cultures, and the fourth year, elective offerings in social studies. At the end of four years, all students have experienced all four curricular areas and fulfilled state social studies requirements.

For another example, the state requires that students spend a certain number of hours in learning and instruction—terms it uses synonymously. Thus, it is not required that students spend all of these hours in a classroom receiving instruction from a teacher. This makes independent study and internships an acceptable option. This approach was particularly useful in relation to physical education, since many of our schools lacked a gymnasium, as well as certified physical education teachers. So, we advanced the notion of "independent study gym," which enabled nearly 75 percent of our students to complete requirements at local YMCAs and Boys and Girls Clubs, or by tutoring games and sports at elementary and middle schools and community recreation facilities. We also gave credit for "life sports" like tennis and golf, practiced by our students on their own outside of school.

We discovered that while schools needed to be in session for five and a half hours a day, the regulation does not require that students be in class for the full five and a half hours each day. Also, lunchtime could count, provided some classes were in session during that time. By creatively interpreting this and other time requirements, we were able to maintain released time to permit the faculty interaction that was so important to our schools.

We tried to protect the freedoms of alternative schools from existing and prospective incursions. One effort that proved very important was undertaken right after Tom Sobol, the progressively minded state commissioner of education, announced his resignation in 1995. We knew that the favorable state climate for the new schools that had developed during his administration might not endure. And so, during the last week he was in office, Deborah Meier, the famous principal of Central Park East Secondary School, and I hastily drafted a waiver for the alternative schools, exempting their students from the state Regents Examinations. We got on a train for Albany and went to see Sobol, who immediately understood how important this could be for innovative schools. He thus gave his approval, despite the absence of the usual six-month review process, and we left his office with the signed waiver. The exemption, and the protection for curricular and assessment departures that it afforded, prevailed for four years.[2]

We tried constantly to steer the implementation of state policies that would affect our schools. For instance, we were able to get the state education department to waive usual certification requirements for our teachers for many years, allowing teachers to teach "out of license" in schools that were not large enough to support full programs for teachers of single disciplines. Our primary concern was to find talented individuals committed to working with youngsters who were often challenging; that they be wholly certified was, to us, secondary. However, even with state education department authorization, such a waiver could become a problem when teacher layoffs threatened, and senior, licensed teachers wanted to claim positions in our schools. But through careful coordination with city officials and the teachers union, the union ultimately became convinced that people shouldn't simply be moved into our schools on the basis of seniority.

When Richard Mills succeeded Sobol as state commissioner of education, he decided to apply increasingly rigid criteria in determining which schools were placed on the state's list of failing schools. With the help of several sympathetic members of the state Board of Regents, we got the commissioner to establish a statewide committee to develop alternative criteria to be used with alternative schools. The criteria that resulted enabled each school to choose its own target goals and to focus and be judged on what it found most important.

As suggested earlier, we also attempted to take full advantage of, and build as fully as possible on, every opportunity that came our way. In some cases, we even manufactured the opportunities. When

[2]It is now, however, as noted in chapter 2, the subject of a lawsuit against the present commissioner brought by a coalition of 35 to 40 alternative schools because of his abrogation of it.

Joe Fernandez became chancellor of New York City Schools, he was looking around for some of the new initiatives urban superintendents are supposed to bring with them. He hit upon the idea of opening new small schools, and we were instrumental in getting the first one under way. It happened this way:

People from Cities in Schools, a national organization with programs in schools across the country, had long wanted to open a school in New York City, but they had never been able to score with the bureaucracy. I learned that the founding board chairman of Cities in Schools had once had contact with Fernandez on a project in Dade County. I drafted a letter for him to send to Fernandez, asking that the chancellor join with him in opening a new school, and the chairman decided to send it. I was relatively certain that I would be asked to draft the response for Fernandez, i.e., the response to the opening letter I had also drafted, and, indeed, this is what happened. In the reply, I identified an underutilized board of education office building and committed the board to doing necessary repairs on it and to assuming planning and start-up costs. Fernandez liked the letter and signed it, and we used it as the basis for bringing Goldman Sachs into the partnership. This move eventually yielded the school, the Metropolitan Corporate Academy, designed to attract students interested in the world of finance.

The alternative schools office played a significant role in the launching of the entire small schools movement that began in New York in the early '90s. Across the city, several of us were very anxious to start a network of new small schools and were able to persuade the Fund for New York Public Education to carry the ball, sponsoring the movement. As it turned out, the fund, which became New Visions, sponsored a number of the new schools; the Center for Collaborative Education—the group that Deborah Meier had launched with her MacArthur "genius" money—sponsored 11; and the city itself, for the first time in almost a century, opened up a number of new schools. These were not schools targeted for unsuccessful students, as the initial alternative schools had been. They were designed for all students who chose to attend them. Yet, most of the schools launched by all three of these sponsors asked to be affiliated with the alternative schools superintendency, and a substantial proportion of them were. But because the chancellor's second in command at the time did not want to see all the credit for the new and innovative programs going to the alternative schools branch of the board, and wanted to establish the High Schools Division as a prime mover in the process, she parceled out a number of them to the High Schools Division instead. (It took the chancellor himself to do it, but several such decisions were eventually reversed in response to strong protest from the schools.)

As a final example of how we exploited every opportunity to permit the number of New York's nontraditional schools to grow, we tried to steer new school proposers with political backing away from applying for New Visions backing—which, of course, was limited—because we knew we could help them win sponsorship from the city. (At the time, new small schools were being sponsored by Deborah Meier's Center for Collaborative Education, by New Visions, and by the city.) In one case, I had been working for five years with the Harlem community school district superintendent and the Boys Choir of Harlem to figure out a way to extend its middle school through 12th grade. Several factors worked in our favor: we had the substantial backing of Citibank; the honorary chair of the Boys Choir board of directors was the mayor's wife; the U.S. Congressman representing Harlem could be counted on to write letters to the chancellor; and we were able to muster support from the president of City College of New York. When we approached the chancellor with this kind of backing, it was not difficult to obtain a go-ahead for the project, which came to be known as the Choir Academy of Harlem.

Still, with all the successes, there were also problems. There is no question that the establishment of the alternative schools superintendency was a great help to accomplishing Alvarado's purposes in establishing it, i.e., strengthening the number, voice, relative freedom, and survival chances of nontraditional schools. Yet, the superintendency is but one of 44 superintendencies in New York City (in addition to five high school borough superintendents, there are 32 community school district superintendents, a special education superintendent, and several others), which does not place it quite at the top of the hierarchical ladder or in a terribly exclusive position. And it is an office that is not integrally tied to others, so it could prove dispensable. It appears to have sufficient political strength to make that unlikely, but this is not guaranteed to last.

Interestingly, however, the sole, serious effort to close the Office of Alternative Schools and return all its schools to the jurisdiction of their boroughs was a total failure. It was undertaken by Alvarado's successor, who set out to reverse a great deal of what his predecessor had done. The alternative school principals quickly organized a protest involving students, parents, and a host of advocates. The culmination of the protest was to occur at a board of education meeting, when principals and advocates were going to speak against ending the superintendency. On the afternoon of the meeting, the deputy chancellor called me to ask if I knew why more than 200 people had placed themselves on the board's agenda to speak. They included the city council president and another council member, the Manhattan borough president, the city clerk, the president of LaGuardia Community College, two top union officials, and a host of others. When I explained what I thought they were going to do, he promised, "If you can guarantee me that not a single one of them will show up, we'll leave the superintendency alone." The principals used a telephone relay to call off the complainers, and I placed myself in the lobby before the meeting, barely managing to head off two officials no one had been able to reach. There have been no other attempts to close down the alternative schools superintendency.

There have, however, been successful efforts to change its direction rather extensively. One afternoon, when I had been in office for 14 years, I received a call from the deputy chancellor, who informed me that as of that day, I was no longer the alternative schools superintendent, and that any effort to challenge this decision would jeopardize the retirement fund I had built up in the system. My successor does not see his mission as I saw mine, and he is thought to operate more as the representative of the administration to his schools, rather than the reverse. I am told that he now has a central office staff of approximately 80. In consequence, the alternative schools superintendency no longer stands in such contrast to other superintendencies and the way they operate.

But even prior to such extreme measures, it was clear that the safety and effectiveness of the alternative schools office was contingent upon the particular chancellor in office. Altogether, in 14 years I served under six chancellors and four interim chancellors. I would say that of the total, four of them were either supportive or at least tolerant of the idea of maintaining a set of nontraditional schools operating rather differently from the rest. Even with the alternative schools superintendency, the fortunes of these schools were very much contingent upon who the chief was, and just how sympathetic he was to letting a group of schools operate differently from the rest. Thus, even though the separate office may appear somewhat secure, there has been no institutionalization of the practices that mark our schools, e.g., the empowerment of teachers, the flattened hierarchy, the small size and personalization, the curricular integration, the performance assessment, the reliance on norms in preference to rules. Nor, even more importantly, has there been any institutionalization of the process we introduced for schools coming into being and shaping themselves.

Given the transitory nature of the administrations of urban chief school officers, we found that as soon as we had really built credibility with a chancellor, he was gone, and we had to start over again. Meanwhile, irrespective of who sits in the chancellor's seat, and doubtless unbeknownst to him, there are almost daily attempts from the bureaucracy he heads to advance the move toward uniformity and standardization. Some way has to be figured out to institutionalize diversity. Otherwise, an inordinate amount of time will have to continue to go to such unnecessary and ridiculous tasks as trying to keep state and city monitors out of nationally acclaimed schools, for fear they will force them to abandon the very practices for which they are winning awards!

CHAPTER 4

Talking the Talk without Walking the Walk: Chicago

Chicago school officials have for seven years offered rhetorical support for small schools but often not much more. A part of the reason has been the politics affecting education in Chicago. The city is a place where two fundamental and not entirely compatible school governance reforms were legislated by the state within a seven-year period. The city itself has also generated a fair number of education reform initiatives of its own. In addition, the influence of outside, non-governmental groups on public schools in Chicago has been remarkable.

The initial reform legislation, in 1988, established school-based management, wherein an elected local school council at each school assumed a number of prerogatives, including considerable authority over curriculum, budget, and the right to hire and fire principals. A 1995 law had the effect of modifying some of this unparalleled authority when it assigned school control to Chicago's mayor, who was given the power to name both a five-member board of trustees (to replace the city's board of education) and a CEO for the schools (to replace the superintendent). The new management team was given broad powers.

The effect of the two pieces of legislation was, in 1988, to set up by far the nation's most *de*centralized school system, and then, in 1995, to lay the groundwork for the considerable *re*centralization that began to appear soon thereafter—and side by side with the local school councils, which continued to operate in each school. As one study put it, "Chicago continues to be among the most radically decentralized school systems in the nation but also has one of the strongest central authorities in its CEO. . . ."[1]

Despite the differences in the two laws, however, they shared one clear commonality: As one analysis put it, "Both . . . reforms are predicated on the notion that change is best achieved through external political influence over and control of professionals. . . ."[2] More specifically, both tended to ignore teachers and had the effect of disempowering them. The 1988 legislation made it quite clear that local school councils making educational as well as governance decisions were each to have 11 members: 8 were to represent parents and the community and 2 were to represent teachers. The 11th member was to be the principal. Thus, teachers' official voice in school decision making was quite limited. Not all teachers saw it this way, however. Many were jubilant that decisions could finally be made so close to home, and some foresaw the possibility of parent- and teacher-designed schools—a number of which came to pass.

The 1995 legislation, however, was another matter, and many feared from the start that it could take away some of the blessings bestowed by the 1988 legislation. The fears were well founded, as this law eventually gave rise to high-stakes tests directing the curriculum; to sanctions, including school reconstitution arrangements requiring the faculties of failing schools to reapply for their positions; and to scripted lessons from the district office for summer school teachers to present to failing students.

At the same time these events were unfolding, however, Chicago—like New York—was experiencing a small schools movement. And while it was inspired and sustained by forces and groups outside the official system, it was not without some official encouragement, though this encouragement was sufficiently self-contradictory at times to cause bewilderment.

---

[1]In Schipps et al., "The Politics of Urban School Reform," 519.

[2]Ibid., 536.

Chicago's last superintendent (just prior to the switch to a CEO) had named a small schools task force. It reported in the spring of 1995, and in the fall, just prior to school's opening, the brand new Reform Board of Trustees named by Chicago's mayor adopted a resolution supporting small schools and establishing "a 'user-friendly' means of encouraging and fostering . . . [them] . . . and of assuring . . . [them] . . . support throughout the administrative structure."[3] The board's resolution characterized what they meant, and what they wanted to see, in this way:

(1) Such schools are small, preferably with enrollment limits of 300 for an elementary school and 500 for a high school. (2) They consist of like-minded teachers and families: "cohesive, self-selected faculties . . . [which] . . . share an educational philosophy" and families which choose this orientation. (3) They are sufficiently autonomous to control key curricular, budgetary, personnel, organizational, and student decisions. (4) They have an agreed-upon focus or theme. (5) Students choose to enroll, and the schools are inclusive rather than selective, including diverse groups and ability/achievement levels. (6) They are effective in preparing and graduating students, aided by a "personalized learning environment and flexibility."[4]

It seemed clear to anyone reading such an official policy statement that having self-selecting teacher groups design their own schools and giving them the freedom to control curricular, budgetary, personnel, and organizational decisions would represent a giant step toward teacher empowerment in almost any of the nation's school districts. So, while it raised the hopes of some school reformers, the resolution also raised the possibility of conflict with provisions in the 1988 reform law. As it turned out, however, the small schools that developed did not conflict nearly as much with the parent and community empowerment represented in the 1988 reform legislation as they did with the measures in the 1995 reform, which came to represent top-down management, with teachers and, sometimes, principals too cast in the role of order takers.

---

[3]In Klonsky, "Small Schools: Creating a Model for School Restructuring in Chicago," 85.

[4]In Azcoitia, *Report and Recommendations on Small Schools in Chicago*, 9.

Chicago's CEO, Paul Vallas, was initially supportive of small schools. Not only did he endorse them but with the encouragement of the Small Schools Coalition, his administration also issued a request for proposals (RFP) for launching 25 new ones. The district was also willing to give the new small schools their own unit numbers that were distinct from the number of the host school in which they were located. This was an important advantage, since the separately assigned number suggested real institutionalization for what could otherwise be treated as a school-within-a-school, existing only at the pleasure of the principal. (Later, the separate unit number enabled small schools to claim credit for student academic achievement that would otherwise have been attributed to a host school.)

But the honeymoon did not last long. Despite the mayor and CEO having blessed small schools,[5] the chief concerns of the Vallas administration quickly crystallized as financial order, standards, and accountability. On such an agenda, the small schools resolution passed by the trustees would be a distraction at best and actually rather out of step with respect to ends as well as means. By the end of 1996, the CEO had declared a moratorium on the creation of new small schools. Since that time, all new small units that have opened have the status of schools-within-schools under the principal's supervision.

Now how, with such an unstable, self-contradictory, and often hostile policy environment, did a small schools movement take place? It was the achievement of a combination of school reform groups, influential business and civic groups, and several large Chicago-based foundations. Since the 1980s, if not before, Chicago has had an astounding number and array of school reform groups. It also has had a number of foundations that supported education reform. Most, if not all, of these groups and their supporters were sympathetic to the 1988 reform legislation, and a number had participated in bringing it about. Many collaborated to bring the Annenberg Challenge grant to Chicago in 1995, an accomplishment that provided further stimulus to the development of small schools. In fact, there was an organization with 125 member groups called

[5]As Mayor Daley said, "The first rule I suggest is, smaller is better." Reported in Spielman, "City High Schools May Get Small," 6.

the Citywide Coalition, and later, the 20-member Chicago School Reform Collaborative, both of which represented the many organizations helping to guide external reform efforts.

These organizations were of many different types. Some were strictly local, grassroots groups concerned about a single school or neighborhood. Others were citywide, some with ethnic identities and equity orientations. There were also several professional education organizations, including Designs for Change, which many credit as the leading force in bringing about the 1988 reform legislation.

So far as small schools are concerned, however, three groups have led the charge. A Small Schools Workshop had been created at the University of Illinois at Chicago in 1991, and it worked to garner support for small schools and aid them in starting and sustaining themselves. This organization, funded by the Joyce and MacArthur foundations, opened eyes to possibilities, first by enabling interested Chicagoans to see what was happening in the small schools in New York. It held a number of public meetings and later helped the venturesome to launch their own small school and schools-within-schools programs.

In the community, the Business and Professional People for the Public Interest (BPI) was a major player in attempting to sell the importance of school size to the broad public. It assisted with the 1995 small schools initiative, and it sponsored several studies and publications intended to show the need for, and accomplishments of, small schools. One major project it spearheaded was a large study, funded by the Joyce Foundation and conducted by Bank Street College of New York, which documented the difference small schools were making within Chicago.

A third organization, Leadership for Quality Education (LQE) also represented the business community and was particularly effective, since its executive director happened to be the brother of one of the two Small Schools Workshop founders.

There was one more major source of help, a $50 million Annenberg Challenge grant, obtained, once again, through the collaborative efforts of a large number of groups. The Chicago public school system was not involved in obtaining the grant, however, and, indeed, its proposal was turned down by those later administering the grant. (As one analyst put it, ". . . the whole Annenberg endeavor . . . was built on the idea that serious district-level change could not be effected from inside the system.")[6] The Annenberg themes to be addressed by proposers were "size, time, and isolation." Thus, small schools were strong prospects in contending for the funds, with their immediate emphasis on size and their frequent focus on collaboration, to combat the typical isolation of teachers. A number of small schools already in existence were successful in obtaining Annenberg monies. And since the grants required networking with at least two other like-minded schools and an external organization, they created a support system for recipients that was of particular value, in light of the absence of support from the system.

It is estimated that Chicago had 30 to 40 small schools as of the early 1990s. Today, with the help of these three groups, plus the Annenberg Challenge grant received in 1995, there are 130 of them, including schools-within-schools. Some say, however, that such figures are overblown, since some of the schools have not been able to obtain the distance and autonomy from their host school to make them genuine. In other cases, insufficient resources have made downsizing into separate faculty and student groups impossible. One high school, for instance, sought to establish separate academies but had to schedule core classes, mixing students from various academies, because there was only one science teacher in the high school of 1,400 students.

Yet, other small schools and schools-within-schools were able to make considerable progress. In 1999, investigators looking at the group that responded to the 1995 RFP reported that their achievement gains (as measured by test scores) had outpaced the district, and their attendance rates exceeded those of the district.[7] And the Bank Street study, which looked more broadly at all of the city's small schools and schools-within-schools concluded:

> These small schools increase student attendance rates and significantly increase student persistence and student performance. More students complete courses, get higher grades,

[6]In Russo, "From Frontline Leader to Rearguard Action," 22.

[7]See Small Schools Coalition, Business and Professional People for the Public Interest, and Leadership for Quality Education, "Small Schools: Hopeful Beginnings."

> and graduate. Further, parents, teachers, students, and community members alike are more satisfied with their schools, believe in them, and want to see them continue to grow.[8]

Most of the existing programs had been established as a result of the efforts of organizations outside the school system. Indeed, the administration's primary preoccupation was with test scores. In fact, maps adorned with colored pins, indicating which schools had reached acceptable scores in math and reading and which had not, covered the walls in the offices of top district officials.

But two system initiatives finally did attempt high school downsizing in the interests of improving achievement. The first was "The Renaissance Project," launched in 1996 in the interests of, as its motto proclaimed, "Transforming Chicago's High Schools for the 21st Century." As Mayor Daley explained it, the city's 75 high schools were to become 750 "smaller, more personal and effective high schools." According to the schedule, the transformation of all 75 high schools was to have been under way, if not completed by 2001.

When response to The Renaissance Project appeared minimal, the issue of what to do with failing schools was difficult to resolve, and the Vallas administration announced the High School Redesign Program. It mandated that high schools be broken down into academies, including one explicitly for all freshmen, and that each school adopt an advisory system for all students. Despite some skepticism about how successful such change could be when mandated from the top, a number of small schools people recognized this program as something quite akin to what they had been urging. Disappointingly, however, reports on the program indicated that it was actually being carried out in only five or six of the city's 75 high schools.

The path has not been an easy one. How did teachers fare, trying to keep small schools alive, given (1) the need to adapt to two conflicting reform orientations imposed by two fairly incompatible reform laws; and (2) shifts in mandates from a district office that sometimes talked the talk but rarely walked the walk? One telling account comes from the principals holding Annenberg Challenge grants, who reported "conflict between their networks' priorities and

[8]In Wasley et al., *Small Schools: Great Strides*, 4.

the priorities of the central office."[9] Founders and teachers in the small schools faced myriad problems. Three groups that had undertaken the considerable task of designing new schools were unable to find space in which to locate so were never able to open at all. One school-within-a-school ceased operating when its students were transferred to another building.[10]

Even while the central administration was calling for school downsizing (with the Renaissance and High School Redesign initiatives), it is said that regional education officers counseled principals not to undertake schools-within-schools! And similar opposition came also from both the city's highest and lowest performing schools, according to the district's chief accountability officer.

Many schools-within-schools were treated more like programs than like schools and were denied any control over their staff or budget. And then came district mandates restricting their ability to operate the programs they had created, e.g., the curricula imposed on schools on probation and the order changing the length of all high school classes throughout the city from 40 to 50 minutes.

Initially, some exemptions were made to accommodate the small schools. Vallas gave Cregier High School permission to have three separate schools with only one principal, a decision that gave rise to the Chicago-coined term *multiplex.* And some small schools were allowed either to do without or to appoint their local school councils. But teacher directors often went unrecognized as official leaders, and there was also interference by unions in some small schools and schools-within-schools, claiming, for instance, that building representatives should decide schedules, not the small schools. In many cases, the small schools encountered considerable difficulty in obtaining the district exemptions necessary to carrying out their missions. Sometimes their external partners could run interference for them, but it was clear that the official granting any exemptions considered them "special favors." Reported one group of investigators, "the . . . central

[9]In Smylie et al., *Getting Started,* 15.

[10]See Small Schools Coalition, Business and Professional People for the Public Interest, and Leadership for Quality Education, "Small Schools: Hopeful Beginnings," 12.

office, many told us, whatever its official line, undercut reform at every opportunity . . ."[11]

Thus, as one observer put it, the district has been "schizophrenic" with respect to small schools and the downsizing of large ones into schools-within-schools. On the one hand, there has been rhetoric and resolutions and RFPs and mandates in favor of such action. On the other hand, there has been little real support provided to the schools by the system. The administration has been too preoccupied with standards and accountability and dealing with failing schools. The focus on size and organizational redesign that downsizing efforts represented was, for CEO Vallas, a digression from the bottom line—the main business of raising test scores. In fact, when asked what had been the major impediments to his efforts to improve the schools, he once replied, "Obstacle number one has been the school reformers. . . ."[12]

Not surprisingly then, the philanthropies and other outsiders could not offer the schools as much help as they needed, even when teachers had been authorized to design a school and find a location for it. The small schools did have a liaison in the central office, but she was the assistant to the chief education officer and she felt highly restricted in what she could do for the small schools effort. Eventually, her title became director of the Office of Special Initiatives (which included small schools plus an array of special projects), but that did not seem to change things much.

The new CEO who replaced Vallas in 2001, Arne Duncan, is of quite a different stripe, however, and there seem to be grounds for new hope. The system has, for the first time, opened an Office of Small Schools, and it is being directed by a former BPI executive, Jeanne Nowaczewski. To date, however, it is not clear that she has been able to substantially change the fortunes of small schools in Chicago.

One other development that may help, however, is the arrival in Chicago of the Gates Foundation, with its small schools program. Gates has given the city $12 million to downsize high schools, and local foundations have matched this sum with $8 million. Anxious to

[11]In Katz et al., "Poking Around," 130.

[12]In Vallas, *Saving Public Schools*, 13.

avoid the predicament of the Annenberg Challenge, with the system and the grant giver at odds and the latter "enmeshed in a very public war between the district and the school-reform community,"[13] the local foundations have insisted on making the school system a party to the efforts being funded. To date, the decision has been reached to attempt to convert five high schools into schools-within-schools.

Perhaps the arrival of this new player, offering additional funds and a new voice—plus the strategy of involving the system, plus the new Office of Small Schools and its leader, plus the new CEO—may collectively make a substantial difference. Hopefully, also, the city's reformers and the schools' CEO will be seeing things similarly, and the schools may find more consistency with respect to hopes, expectations, and demands. Indeed, the system may finally begin walking the walk. Certainly the history recounted here suggests that the support extended to small schools by the district was for years little more than rhetoric. And the instability generated by changing laws and school administrations provided a context and policy environment it was difficult to count on.

[13]In Russo, "From Frontline Leader to Rearguard Action," 25.

CHAPTER 5

Philadelphia: The Superintendent's Baby

Philadelphia was really the nation's first city to launch a systemwide downsizing effort, which began in 1988 and was aimed at all its high schools. It remains the only city that has since set out to assure the downsizing of all large schools at all grade levels.

The initial effort began with a "massive restructuring" attempt under the leadership of the Philadelphia Schools Collaborative, a partnership formed among the School District of Philadelphia, comprehensive high schools, and the Philadelphia Federation of Teachers.[1] Constance Clayton, who was superintendent at the time, announced that, as a means of reforming secondary education, all 22 of the city's high schools would be divided into schools-within-schools (called "charters" in Philadelphia, as suggested by Albert Shanker, then president of the American Federation of Teachers). Middle schools were divided into "houses."

Although implementation of charters was quite uneven across the city, several schools took on the challenge with enthusiasm, creating dynamic programs like Crossroads at Simon Gratz High

[1]In McMullan, *Trends in Student Achievement among Students Enrolled in Philadelphia's Comprehensive High Schools.*

School. So, there was some history and accomplishment related to the creation of small, semiautonomous schools-within-schools when Superintendent David Hornbeck succeeded Clayton in 1994, even though Superintendent Clayton had stopped short of mandating the charters, thereby leaving the decision to majority vote on the part of each school's faculty.

Hornbeck's "Children Achieving" program, however, made downsizing a key and a required plank. The superintendent mandated that any school in Philadelphia, at any grade level, with an enrollment exceeding 400 students be divided into schools-within-schools, or what he called "small learning communities" (and others came to call "SLC," or, collectively, SLCs, pronounced "slix"). His effort provides a good example of an attempt to bring a substantial organizational restructuring to scale from the start.

By the 1995-96 school year, there were 132 SLCs in high schools alone, with more than 90 percent of the total high school population enrolled in them. It should be noted, however, that a number of these SLCs were the charters earlier established by the collaborative.[2]

Hornbeck spoke repeatedly of the need to pursue his 10-point Children Achieving program "all at the same time." The other 9 points were arriving at new standards of performance and new accountability measures; shrinking the central bureaucracy in favor of more decentralized decision making at the school level; offering professional development for all staff and adequate resources for all schools; organizing schools into 22 clusters or complexes, each representing a high school and its feeder middle and elementary schools; establishing individual school partnerships with at least one external institution or organization; and establishing a local school council with some real decision-making power at each school.

Thus, in Philadelphia, which one official spoke of as "the land of small learning communities," policy appeared to strongly favor the downsizing effort. Principals were empowered with more budgetary decisions and the right not to fill some positions in the interests of other priority expenditures. But in the opinion of many, Children Achieving did not empower teachers—only the teacher coordinator of each SLC. These coordinators, as a group, were perceived to have

[2]Ibid.

gained authority. It was mandated that there be a teacher coordinator for each SLC and that they be released from at least one class. (Some were released from as many as three.) But the coordinator role differed considerably from school to school. Some principals wanted the teacher coordinators of SLCs to function as instructional leaders; others did not. Some were expected to function as disciplinarians; others were not. Since principals were left with so much discretion, some SLCs were relatively autonomous and free to arrive at their own decisions. A good many, however, were not.

Hornbeck began with an accountability system, preparing standards and developing a school Performance Responsibility Index, and the needed professional development and support followed very shortly thereafter. It was mandated that the teachers of a small learning community have a common meeting time during the school day. And there were efforts to provide professional development, with reimbursement to teachers for time spent outside the school day. As the initial funding dwindled, however, so did the support. The result was that later, teachers indicated dissatisfaction with the kind and amount of help provided.

A list from the superintendent's office of the "Essential Characteristics/Standards" for the small learning communities specified that each should (1) have its own unifying theme, (2) extend across several grade levels, (3) be empowered with the "authority and resources to design [its] own instructional program," and (4) have "sufficient time for teachers to engage in meaningful planning and professional development."

A large number of small learning communities were, in fact, formed during Hornbeck's administration. Perhaps because of the prior history there, SLCs appeared to be more extensive and fully developed in the high schools, although they were more popular in the middle schools. The idea was not always applied, particularly in the elementary schools, as the superintendent's essential characteristics and standards would have had it. For instance, in the second year of the program, in a number of elementary schools the unifying theme for each SLC was a color. So, a school might have a red small learning community, a blue one, and a yellow one in the building. Obviously, this is not a theme around which an instructional program can be organized, any distinctiveness can emerge, or any sense of affiliation can grow. In the high schools, the themes were often more distinctive, but many turned out to be career themes bringing a strong threat of tracking, e.g., business or cosmetology.

Moreover, it was not universally the case that teachers were given the right to choose the colleagues with whom they would collaborate. This limited the extent to which the small learning communities represented a common orientation or interest among their faculties. In addition, not all students were able to choose their small learning community. This seems particularly unfortunate for students at the high school level, where, for example, those interested in engineering might be assigned to an SLC with a health services theme. However, themes did not always pervade the curriculum, so a poor match between a student and a theme was not always very pronounced. As evaluators put it, "There was tremendous variation in the salience of unifying themes for small learning communities in the high schools. All of the high school small learning communities had a focus, often career-related, but frequently the focus had little application to what took place daily in the classrooms."[3]

The high school small learning communities also suffered from what evaluators called "roster integrity," meaning that just because a student was assigned to a particular SLC did not mean that all of his or her courses would be taken within that SLC or taught by teachers assigned to that learning community. In fact, some students had only one or two classes in the SLC to which they were assigned. Researchers found that major achievement outcome differences hinged upon the number of courses students took in their own SLC.[4] So, even though it might be said that a number of SLCs were established in Philadelphia in a several year period, there were vast differences in the extent to which each was implemented and thus to how they could benefit students.

Superintendent Hornbeck was well aware of the problems and the incompleteness with which many schools were implementing the Children Achieving agenda. He was convinced that that would begin to change at a faster pace during the 2000-01 school year, when each small learning community would be assigned its own administrative

---

[3]In Christman, *Guidance for School Improvement in a Decentralizing System*, 23.
[4]See McMullen et al., *Charters and Student Achievement*.

unit number, rather than remaining submerged and anonymous within the building's unit number. This would make it possible to hold each SLC accountable for its success, which was defined by a Performance Responsibility Index score computed from test results (60 percent); student and staff attendance (20 percent); and student promotion and persistence, i.e., not dropping out (20 percent).[5]

Hornbeck's ambitious "all at once" plan was funded by a $50 million Annenberg Challenge grant that was supplemented by a locally raised $100 million. He also later anticipated $300 million from the state to help underwrite the extensive restructuring effort. That amount never materialized.[6] And the state funding received, even for regular school operation, was insufficient, due to three things that were happening simultaneously: Philadelphia's school enrollments were increasing; its students and their families, including the new ones, were increasingly needful of social services; and school revenues were declining.[7] In 1993, the legislature had frozen the state's school aid formula, so there could be no increases. Through the 1990s, the state's contribution to Philadelphia schools had been diminishing. According to *Education Week*'s "Quality Counts" report, the state rated only a C- or a D with respect to funding equity, or its attempt to offset what wealthier communities can pay to support their schools with contributions to poorer ones.[8] Even though the local tax rate in Philadelphia was above 12 percent, as compared to half that in some of the state's wealthy districts, the city was running a large annual deficit of several hundred million dollars.

In 1998, Hornbeck threatened to close the schools before the end of the school year unless the state increased their funding. The legislature responded with a law allowing state takeover of any district in educational or financial "distress." Despite extensive

---

[5]See Innerst, "Grant Brings High Hopes, Modest Gains to Philadelphia School Reform."

[6]See Christman, *Guidance for School Improvement in a Decentralizing System.*

[7]In Philadelphia Schools Collaborative, Final Report, 14.

[8]According to *The Philadelphia Public School Notebook*, the gap between the state's wealthiest and poorest districts was almost $200,000 per classroom. In *Philadelphia Public School Notebook*, "Philadelphia School Fundings: Questions and Answers."

borrowing on the part of the district, there simply wasn't enough money to do the job.[9]

The deficit, plus Hornbeck's repeated demands for additional funds, put the superintendent in constant contention with state officials. Finally, Hornbeck led in the filing of a suit against the state of Pennsylvania on behalf of "Philadelphia Students, community organizations, and Philadelphia public bodies and officials, including the Mayor, the Board of Education, and the Superintendent of Schools." The grounds for the suit were violation of the Civil Rights Act of 1964: it charged that the civil rights of minority students were being violated by the underfunding of Philadelphia schools.[10]

Of course, the state's legislature and governor were incensed over the suit. In fact, it was not until the city's school board agreed to postpone it that an emergency state appropriation enabled Philadelphia to keep its schools open during the summer of 2000 and avoid a state takeover. (The mayor predicted the schools would run out of money in July, a situation that would trigger a state takeover by virtue of the new law cited earlier).[11] But Hornbeck saw the handwriting on the wall and realized it would be impossible to operate, much less to reform, the city's schools with the sort of fiscal support he was receiving. He resigned in June and left office August 15, 2000.

Part of the problem had undoubtedly been the city-versus-state struggle that plagues large urban centers everywhere—e.g., New York City versus New York State, Chicago versus Illinois—with state officials pessimistic about the possibility of fixing urban schools at any cost. Part of it also was a disagreement in priorities between the governor, Tom Ridge, Hornbeck, and Philadelphia's new mayor, John Street. Another part of it was the mayor's hope that with a less contentious strategy, more could be accomplished with the state. He supported Hornbeck's program but felt that more amicable dealings might help. But the problems were broader than political strategy, or a Republican state government versus Democratic city officials. There were within-system problems as well. Some of these were primarily structural in nature, while others had more to do with policy.

---

[9]See Gewertz, "It's Official: State Takes Over Philadelphia Schools."

[10]In *Philadelphia Public School Notebook,* "Federal Court to Hear Bias Case," 15.

[11]See Johnston, "Settlement Averts School Shutdown in Philadelphia".

Surveys have shown that the small learning communities were the most popular part of the Children Achieving package with teachers.[12] Yet there were teachers in high schools who continued to be opposed to the downsizing and who felt that the SLCs interfered with departments, and thus with academic achievement. In fact, secondary school teachers turned out to be more negative on virtually all of Hornbeck's reform agenda than were elementary and middle school teachers.[13]

Another aspect of the problem was undoubtedly the "all at once" strategy. This meant that each school, and the district as a whole, were trying simultaneously to build an enormous amount of new infrastructure: small learning communities, local school councils, clusters, and partnerships with local institutions and organizations. At the same time, both were trying to shift to standards-based instruction in classrooms and to receive professional development when that was proffered. Given that the superintendent's restructuring agenda was so comprehensive, perhaps the "all at once" strategy was ill-advised, even though the breadth of the plan is probably one of its virtues.

There was difficulty with the Philadelphia Federation of Teachers over seniority and transfer rights, and the union found the powers over budget and personnel assigned to local school councils incompatible with the collective bargaining agreement. They had earlier taken issue with the impact of the high school charters on department heads. There were also conflicts between the powers over their own instructional programs assigned to SLCs and the powers of the local school council. (Moreover, a local school council was not required to include a representative of every one of the school's small learning communities, so some were not represented.)

The Children Achieving plan resulted in new roles and responsibilities and shifts in power, and, of course, there were concerns about these. Principals didn't like the new accountability assigned them and were concerned about the new cluster arrangements, which substituted for what had been six regions. The regional administrators, of course, were unhappy with their replacement, and central administrators were concerned about decentralization. Some critics said

---

[12]See Christman, *Guidance for School Improvement in a Decentializing System.*

[13]Ibid.

Hornbeck's new structure with the clusters wasn't decentralization at all, and, in fact, just created a new, even larger set of administrators with supervisory powers.[14]

So despite the fact that SLCs were the superintendent's "baby" and a key part of his Children Achieving plan, and despite the fact that Hornbeck made elaborate efforts to eliminate all the loopholes and help teachers achieve while raising expectations for them, his administration lasted only six years. This was longer than the average term for an urban superintendent but not long enough to complete his extensive plans. There was some real accomplishment with respect to student attendance and achievement, but as we have suggested, there were school people who were not enthusiastic about his plans. As time passed, he faced an increasingly hostile policy environment as imposed from the state capitol.

Thus, it appears that not even a superintendent can assure a positive policy environment for reform. Had he been able to retain the support, especially the financial support, of the legislature, Hornbeck might have been able to realize his ambitious program. It was carefully planned and sequenced. But superintendents too are surrounded by a policy environment and in this case, one that became progressively less supportive.

[14]See Innerst, "Grant Brings High Hopes, Modest Gains to Philadelphia School Reform."

Chapter 6

Pilots on the Fringes: Boston

The somewhat limited small schools movement in Boston has been unique. It is the only place where small schools have been launched explicitly to 'pilot' innovation for the district. The schools also began in a most unusual way. In 1994, as a way of responding to the many charter schools then opening and of demonstrating that the "Establishment" could welcome innovation, the Boston Teachers Union proposed to the superintendent that the Boston Public Schools open a set of "in-district charters." That is, the teachers union recommended the launching of a group of schools free of district regulations and collective bargaining agreement constraints. As some put it, the purpose was to "preempt" the charter schools.

The superintendent, Lois Harrison Jones, accepted the proposal (although reportedly without much enthusiasm), and it was agreed that the city would sponsor an undetermined number of "Pilot" schools. Her successor, Tom Payzant, has gone along with the idea, and, in fact, has, at times, talked of increasing the number of Pilot schools. But they have remained largely peripheral to his agenda. The central office liaison with the Pilot schools was extremely sympathetic to the Pilot schools and a committed advocate, but he lacked the authority to help them very much. His replacement is reportedly less of an advocate and has even less authority.

When the Pilot schools were launched in 1994, there were initially some rough times. The majority of the schools found they had to fight to receive the full pupil allotments to which the agreement entitled them. There were union problems with custodians and secretaries. There were payroll problems, and there was concern that the memorandum of agreement allowed the superintendent to close a Pilot school on 30 days notice. The system became concerned as to whether the Pilots had been enrolling their share of special education students. And the Pilots, like many innovative schools elsewhere, wanted to serve classified students on an inclusionary basis, ignoring their classified status but still claiming the extra funding provided for these students. There was also trouble over other matters, such as report cards, since the narratives that Pilots preferred didn't fit on the system's computers. The problems were so severe that the first time it was announced that Pilot schools could become chartered, five out of the seven then existing applied. (Two were chartered but also remained Pilot schools.)

As a consequence of such difficulties, the Pilots, now grown to number 11, decided to band together to deal with the system. They asked the Center for Collaborative Education, a nonprofit organization in Boston that works with a number of schools interested in progressive reform, to represent them. Dan French, who heads the office, is an experienced Boston schoolman and former state education official. He has been able to smooth the way, as well as to obtain what teachers in many schools would consider remarkable concessions. He, along with the Pilot school directors, typically negotiates directly with the superintendent and the deputy superintendent.

Pilot schools are able to select and hire their own staff and create their own staffing arrangements, instead of having to use district formulas. By reducing the number of electives, and by having teachers assume some staff roles (e.g., scheduling and coaching), they have been able to lower pupil-teacher ratios in regular classes. Additionally, by taking on teacher aides, part-time staff, and interns, they have been able to ensure the presence of more than one adult in many classrooms at any given moment, thus lowering the student-to-staff ratio to 15 to one.[1]

[1]See Center for Collaborative Education, *How Boston Pilot Schools Use Freedom Over Budget, Staffing, and Scheduling to Meet Student Needs.*

And all of this is done without extra funding from the district. Pilot schools receive the same per-pupil amounts that are allotted to other Boston public schools, plus the cost of nonessential services, which, by agreement, the Pilot schools can opt not to receive from the district. These include contracted services, coaches, school-to-career services, and other programs. This adds approximately $400 per pupil to the Pilot school budgets. They also attempt to supplement their budgets by obtaining external funds. The Center for Collaborative Education serves as the fiscal agent and administers the funds received by 10 of the 11 Pilot schools from philanthropies, corporations, and partners. This gives them direct and immediate access to the monies they have obtained.

The Pilots also have a great deal of curricular and scheduling autonomy. The former often leads to dual teaching arrangements. The latter not only permits the flexibility to change the schedule during the year—but also to build in a great deal of professional development time for collaborative teacher meetings. (One Pilot has built in weekly three-hour meetings of the full faculty, weekly two-hour meetings of the staffs of the two school "Houses," one weekend retreat during the school year, five days at the end of the school year, and ten days at the beginning of the year.)[2]

As one Pilot school director summed up the freedom,

> . . . the major autonomy, for me, is from the constraints that feel irrational. . . . What that does is take what is probably the most complicated and challenging . . . task that we've got in front of us . . . this business of educating urban children. . . . And give you some sense of control.[3]

The Pilot schools have been free to create their own assessments, and all have done so. If left responsible for administering only these assessments, their curricular freedom would be substantial. But Pilot school students, like all other Boston public school students, must take state tests, and they are demanding: on initial administration, 91 percent of the city's high school students failed the math exam and some 60 percent failed the English exam.

---

[2]Ibid.

[3]Ibid., i.

In addition, Boston has devised its own standards, which it views as "the central reform measure driving school improvement. . . ."[4] Student learning in Boston has been assessed by the state at intervals (tests in grades 4, 8, and 10) and the city administers its own tests in all other grades, 3 to 11. It remains to be seen whether this state-city test sponsorship pattern will change in the wake of the federal No Child Left Behind program.

Boston's exams are part of Superintendent Payzant's comprehensive reform plan for Boston's Schools called "Focus on Children." Its primary goal is the improvement of teaching and learning for all children, and it calls for "Whole-School Change" in all 132 of the city's schools. Although the plan alludes to changes in organizational structure and the provision of safe, nurturing schools and external partnerships, the focus is on the curricular and instructional change necessary to enable students to meet the city's standards and assessment program.

The Whole-School Change effort has been supported by a strong emphasis on professional development for teachers and principals. There is a mentorship program for new teachers, a lead teacher program, and considerable development and training for all. An Annenberg grant helped finance these efforts, and four different groups of schools each received four years of intensive support. All of Boston's public schools have now been involved in one or another of these four cohorts—all except the Pilot schools. As the Boston Plan for Excellence reports, in Pilot schools, "reform work is managed within their own network."[5]

That members of that network have been successful could hardly be denied. The Pilot Schools serve a population that is generally representative of the Boston Public Schools. There are fewer low-income students in Pilot elementary schools than in other public schools, but in middle and high schools, the figures are approximitely the same. And Pilot high schools enroll significantly more African Amerian students than do non-Pilot high schools. But the Pilot schools have among the highest attendance rates in the city, the longest

---

[4]In Boston Public Schools, *Focus on Children*, 44.

[5]In Boston Plan for Excellence in the Public Schools, *Fact Sheet*.

waiting lists, the lowest suspension rates, and the fewest student transfers. Their students perform at or above system averages on the state exams, with three of the four Pilot high schools outranked only by the selective exam schools. Two of the three Pilot elementary schools' students outscore other Boston public school students at the high levels and have fewer failing students than do other schools.[6]

Although the city's comprehensive plan states that as a part of the Whole-School Change process, schools should "review models for restructuring large schools into smaller learning communities,"[7] for some time it was unclear just how much was being done to really encourage such downsizing. Several years ago, a task force on high school restructuring was established in the collective bargaining agreement, and it has recommended the smaller units. An Office of High School Restructuring was set up, and its coordinator met periodically with secondary school principals and headmasters to encourage them to divide their schools into small learning communities. But the job was a staff role only in relation to the schools, and after several years of such sessions, its young incumbent was not very optimistic about the prospects for downsizing. She concluded that the cultural change it was her assignment to bring about could occur only following the imposition of structural change. An $8 million grant recently received from the Carnegie Foundation to establish small learning communities may provide some inspiration and movement in that direction. And, indeed, the city's 12 comprehensive high schools have now been mandated to establish schools-within-schools, each with a maximum of 500 students. Not all of these units may be themed, however, and to date it appears that not all of their students and teachers will arrive in the units as a matter of choice.

Meanwhile, save for some elementary schools, Boston's small schools remain limited to its 11 Pilot schools. The teachers of one small comprehensive high school of 700 students—Boston High School—have voted to become a Pilot school. And according to the collective bargaining agreement, two new elementary schools now

---

[6]See Center for Collaborative Education, *Executive Summaries of CCE Reports on the Boston Pilot Schools Network.*

[7]In Boston Public Schools, *Focus on Children,* 24.

being planned will be Pilots. Thus, the total may grow to 14 in the next several years.

As much of the above suggests, however, within the Boston public school system the Pilots have been quite peripheral. They have not entirely regretted being on the periphery. It has given them the autonomy that they need to sustain truly innovative programs: as indicated earlier, they are able to control their own hiring and budgetary allocations, purchasing, school organization, and curriculum. But the autonomy seems to have come with a price.

The Pilots have had some positive effects on the school system. For instance, their assessment systems are now being looked at by other high schools. The Quality Review Process that was worked out by the Pilot schools was later adopted by the system for all Boston public schools. And there is a proposal to reward clearly effective schools with the same budgetary freedom Pilots get. This idea may seem a bit turned around from the Pilot schools' vantage point, since they might well claim it to be the ineffective schools that are more in need of such freedom. Still, the message was received, at least in part.

But by and large, the Pilot schools are not being used as the ideas sources they were intended to be. According to the Comprehensive Reform Plan, the Pilot schools were "to explore models of educational excellence which will help foster widespread educational reform throughout all of the Boston Public Schools."[8] But just how to stand as such a model has been something of a sore point. District officials are unhappy that the Pilot schools are not sharing their innovations more widely. The schools, on the other hand, feel that they have been given little recognition. They also tend to feel that while they are willing to describe and exhibit what they do, it is not their obligation to advertise or create the occasions for such sharing. They are also not sure how anxious others are to learn about what they are doing, since some of those in other Boston schools hold the Pilots to be simply "a different breed," working under quite different circumstances from their own, and hence not relevant for them. Thus, the inspiration these schools might offer remains quite circumscribed.

[8]Ibid., 27.

Chapter 7

A Principal-Inspired Set of Schools-within-Schools: Kapaa Elementary School

Kapaa, Hawaii, is a small town on the island of Kauai. Although remote, with the venture described here antedating the small schools movement by several years, it is of interest in two regards: the policy environment the elementary school principal managed to establish within the school, and the systemwide policies the school faced externally.

Kapaa's oversized elementary school enrolls the children of the town and the surrounding semirural area. A majority of these youngsters are of native Hawaiian and Filipino background—two ethnic groups that correlate with low academic achievement in Hawaii. Within the last decade, the percentage of students at the school who are eligible for full or reduced-cost lunches has moved from a third to more than half.

Early in 1989, Clifton Bailey was named principal of Kapaa Elementary School—the fourth principal to be assigned there in five years. He was appalled at what he found, including ability grouping beginning in the first or second grade, and fourth through sixth graders receiving daily, 50-minute lessons in each discipline, in rigidly specified sequence. So, he was searching for the means to launch change. The community was also ready for it. A parent/teacher exchange meeting concluded that the 1,500-student school was too large,[1] and that it lacked a sense of community as well as communication—between grade levels, between teachers and parents, and between teachers and students.

Thus, the new principal was pleased when a small but vigorous group of reform-minded parents wanted to bring a visiting professor over from Honolulu to talk with them about reform. The group of 10-12 parents met with the visitor, who told them about schools-within-schools and the reforms they make possible. The audience was enthusiastic but uncertain about how to proceed. The problem was largely solved, however, by the next morning's local newspaper.

The same day of the speaker's visit, the chairman of the state senate's education committee had visited Kapaa Elementary School and told a reporter that the school was too large and ought to be divided into three separate schools. The threat of such dire change as creating three separate schools made faculty uneasy and immediately galvanized a number of parents (at least some of whom might otherwise never have been enthusiasts) in favor of schools-within-schools.

The senator managed to obtain some special funding to help support the venture, and the principal invited teacher groups to self-select and propose schools with a theme, or an articulating focus, of their choice. After much hesitation, and a promise from the principal that he would remain at the school for at least three years, two groups somewhat timidly stepped forward.

In the next several years, six more did so, with the result that by 1993, Kapaa Elementary School consisted entirely of schools-within-schools. It subsequently became five, due to the reduction of the school's enrollment (caused by the reassignment of the entire sixth grade to a newly built school) and the need to align upper- and lower-grade SWSs. But the five remain as of this writing, despite the sudden and untimely death of Principal Bailey in January 2001.

Looking first at the school policy environment within which the schools-within-schools work, teachers have experienced strong support of various sorts. In Hawaii teachers' experience is extensively that of orders takers, and thus they needed a lot of help in creating their own programs and establishing their own school climates. Anticipat-

[1]Hawaii's average school size, at all grade levels, is among the largest in the nation.

ing this, Bailey used a part of the grant money he continued to obtain to create a new role in the school, that of "teacher facilitator." (And when grant funds were no longer available, he used Title I and state 'special needs' funds to support this role.) The purpose was to provide each SWAS with the sort of help its teachers wanted, be it curriculum design, locating materials, special professional development or training opportunities, or grant proposal writing.

The first teacher facilitators were two outstanding young women who wanted a job-share situation. Both brought extraordinary talents and experience in professional development, curriculum, and instructional strategies, and both contributed a lot more than the half time for which they were paid. The position has since been filled by a former teacher at Kapaa who has continued the tradition and provided major boosts for the teachers' efforts. (At a recent juncture, when the faculty was consulted about continuing the teacher facilitator role, they strongly favored doing so.)

The principal also made the SWSs his primary concern. He divided the functions among himself and his two vice principals in such fashion that he was running the innovation and the VPs were handling most of the necessary maintenance/management functions for the school. Thus, the principal remained clearly the leader, protector, and advocate of the new arrangement, while at the same time nurturing community partnerships and seeking other forms of external support.

Those within the SWSs experienced quite a lot of support especially from the principal and the teacher facilitator. Several years into the restructured arrangement, teachers confirmed on anonymous surveys that they were being encouraged to stretch and grow (98 percent), that the principal took a personal interest in their professional development (88 percent), and that he encouraged them to assume the risks associated with taking on new instructional strategies (93 percent).[2] They also confirmed that they had been empowered

[2]This survey was part of an evaluation of the Kapaa SWSs effort conducted in 1994. The survey was adapted from the one designed in Chicago by the Consortium on Chicago School Research and later administered to all of Chicago's elementary school teachers. The benefits reported by Kapaa's teachers substantially exceeded those reported by Chicago's teachers following the adoption of school-based management in that city. See Raywid, "Mapping Progress toward Restructuring: One School's Story."

with respect to curriculum determination and materials selection (93 percent), the setting of behavioral standards (77 percent), and the determination of student progress (80 percent). Thus, it seems safe to say that as their faculties experienced it, the SWSs were operating in quite a positive and supportive policy environment. How did the principal fashion it so? Here are some of the steps he took.

There were a number of supports and incentives nurturing the SWSs structure and teachers. In addition to the teacher facilitators, who helped individual SWSs pursue grant possibilities, the principal also sought and obtained funding. This was used in part to enable a SWAS that wanted to bring in a developer to do so, or to enable SWAS staff to visit a mentor and site. Each SWAS received a lump sum based on enrollment, but each was encouraged to consider the overall needs of their program and could request support beyond the enrollment allotment.

To encourage innovation, Bailey also changed the way in which the special needs monies due the school (largely from Title I funds and similar state funding) were distributed. Under the mantle of "equity," the tradition at the school had been to allot these funds to each classroom according to enrollment count. Bailey changed the allocation procedure and instead requested proposals indicating plans for use of the funds for promising, innovative purposes. He then sought to establish a schoolwide committee, composed largely of teachers, who were to make recommendations regarding the proposals received. When the proposals did not seem to warrant funding, the money was to go into technology and extra staffing to reduce class size.

He also sought to build leadership capacity among teachers. He established a schoolwide leadership team consisting of the resource teachers and one representative from each SWAS, and this group became a decision-making body. Its members were also given a small pay differential, which state officials questioned, and to which they acceded only upon submission of a formal justification.

As all of this indicates, teachers within Kapaa's SWSs worked in an extremely positive policy environment that provided support for their work as well as incentives to enhance it yet further. So far as the principal was concerned, however, the policy environment in which he worked outside the school was nowhere as supportive.

In 1989, the same year Bailey latched onto the SWSs idea, the Hawaii state legislature passed a bill designed to stimulate school-based management throughout the state. It was not a mandate (which would have approached the self-contradictory), but schools were strongly encouraged by the law, and then by the state board of education, which had backed it, to submit letters of intent to establish school-based management (or, actually, Hawaii's version, which was called *school/community-based management*, or SCBM). Pressure was immediately exerted on each of the state's seven district superintendents to see that their districts were 100 percent, with all schools declaring SCBM intent. (The district superintendents are actually just representatives of the state superintendent. Hawaii has a unitary governance system whereby the state directly controls all schools.)

Bailey's district superintendent was known to favor reform, so she was not negatively disposed toward his project. On the other hand, the pressure exerted on her to have him move in the direction of SCBM dulled any inclinations she might have had toward extending support to him in the course he had chosen to pursue. Bailey was reluctant to go into SCBM because he thought it would divert energy and attention from a strategy he felt was much more likely to expedite classroom change. There may also have been some question in his mind as to whether an SCBM council in this working class community could be nontraditional enough to authorize the move to SWSs. He consulted teachers formally, by vote, and the parent/teacher organization. The school community was unanimous in the decision to postpone the SCBM process. Thus, he resisted submission of a letter of intent for seven or eight years, before finally succumbing. By the time Bailey sent his letter, he felt that the SWSs were sufficiently well established that the distraction of SCBM would not be as serious as it might have been earlier, when they were just getting under way. In addition, by that time, the SWSs had managed to obtain considerable parent participation and support. And finally, the state had arranged the incentives in a manner comparable to what he, himself, had done inside his school: state funds available to schools for innovative purposes were given only to those that had become SCBM schools.

A much graver impediment to the SWSs was the collective bargaining agreement entitling any tenured teacher in the state to replace any probationary teacher in the SWSs, even though the "probie" had participated in planning and undergone extensive training as part of a team. Still today, each probationary teacher thus represents an unprotected investment on the part of a SWAS. So, each spring, when the lists of available positions are posted, morale drops—and probationary teachers begin worrying about being replaced. The SWSs begin worrying about who might be placed on their teams and whether a newcomer would prove compatible and supportive or a poor team player or even a saboteur. (At the time of Bailey's sudden death, discussion was under way in the Kapaa SCBM council about submitting a waiver petition to retain probationary teachers who had been trained in the particular curriculum and instructional strategies specific to a given SWAS.)

There have been recurring problems with the state department of education due to the fact that Kapaa is not doing things as other schools are doing them. For instance, a stipend for teachers performing leadership roles was questioned. And the school's proposal for Comprehensive School Reform Development (CSRD) funds was turned down, since the SWSs—laudably—wanted to go in different directions from one another.

Action on the part of the state legislature, which is far more active in setting school policy than in many states, has also posed difficulties for Kapaa. For instance, its raising of the student-to-teacher ratio led to the loss of a position in each SWAS and threatened continuation of one of the programs.

Perhaps because his SWSs venture became well known throughout the state and beyond as a creative and successful reform that had made a difference, no steps were taken by the district superintendent or her successors to terminate Bailey's restructured arrangements at Kapaa. But despite being recognized as a visionary educator and a reform leader in the community, and, to some extent, on the mainland, his considerable accomplishments were never officially acknowledged by his district, the state superintendent, or the department of education.

CHAPTER 8

International High School

International High School in Queens, New York, has spent most of its almost 20 years engaged in an intense, sustained search for a viable environment in which to conduct its own affairs. It was, from its founding in 1985, an official member of the alternative schools superintendency in New York City. In 1999, International and its sister school, Middle College High School, became the first NYC high schools to be accorded charter status. Two years later, they became the first schools to renounce charter status and enter a long dreamed of *Learning Zone*, again under the aegis of the NYC Board of Education but with unique promises of curricular and organizational autonomy.

International's history is replete with the frustrations and indignities of coping with a large urban bureaucracy. Yet the school has been relentless in its struggle to determine for itself the instruction and assessment of its students and the ways in which its faculty is organized and governed. It has done so through a combination of political savvy, creativity in interpreting (or bending or breaking) rules, public confrontation when necessary, and unusual internal cohesion.

International was established specifically to serve students from other countries who arrived in this country with little or no command of English. A majority of its students also come from poverty-level homes. Yet its success rate in engaging, retaining, and graduating students and sending them on to higher education compares favorably with that of the top NYC high schools. Its dropout rate has been as low as 1 percent and its college attendance rate has been as high as 96 percent.

Even on the standardized New York State Regents Exams, which all students were required to pass, beginning in 2000, International's students have met with surprising success. Prior to that time, International had prepared its students solely for the sophisticated performance assessments that were the school's trademark. The school had, in fact, led a very public—but ultimately unsuccessful—fight against the sweeping Regents requirements.

* * * * *

For a school that has taken such an independent path, International did not begin far outside the mold. At the outset, there were the traditional eight-period days, 40-minute periods, and "teachers in the front of the room," as the staff describes it. But soon, the faculty recognized that if they were to have any chance of succeeding with their challenging, at-risk population, they would need to organize themselves differently. They lengthened class time, increased interdisciplinary work, and instituted peer review among the staff. Perhaps most significantly, they invested great energy in developing comprehensive systems of performance assessment for their students. The school began to be noticed as a dynamic, innovative, yet steady institution that served its community reliably and well. Its policies, as they developed, were written up clearly and disseminated widely. Its founding principal, Eric Nadelstern, became a prominent voice among his peers in the burgeoning small schools movement of the '90s. Other schools emulated International's peer review and performance assessment practices, and new "international" high schools in Manhattan and Brooklyn (and, most recently, The Bronx) adopted many of International's methods.

When it was part of a small, protected network in the Alternative School superintendency in the '80s—and even in the boom days of the early '90s—International was able, for the most part, to chart its own course. The huge New York City bureaucracy was able to ignore some of International's divergences from prescribed practice, partly because the small number of similarly inclined schools did not threaten the hegemony of the larger system. Chancellors Fernandez and Cortines encouraged a certain amount of innovation, and the various reform networks, under the Annenberg umbrella, provided moral and some logistical support.

But International was never entirely free of the tangle of confining rules and energy-draining procedures that characterized the board of education, and the situation became even more challenging in the late '90s. The new chancellor, Rudy Crew, began an effort to reclaim authority for the central administration. And, to complicate matters further for schools that attempted to tailor instruction and assessment to individual students, the standards movement and its companion, high-stakes testing, had taken a firm foothold.

By now, there were several hundred self-declared small schools in New York City, and schools like International could no longer assume that their variances would not threaten the larger system. International and its peer schools were feeling increasingly intense pressure toward centralization and standardization and began to worry about holding on to even the most basic elements of their individuality.

Meanwhile, charter schools had arrived in New York. Rapidly gaining national momentum in the previous decade, charters promised a high degree of autonomy in exchange for increased accountability. In December 1998, with little advance notice, the legislature authorized charter start-ups and conversions in New York State. Chancellor Crew, originally dismissive of the charter concept, reversed himself after the proposal became law and offered New York City as a chartering agent for selected schools, with the city to share authority with the state. International was among a few invited to consider joining the first wave of charter conversions.

A decision needed to be made, and proposals submitted, in short order. Nadelstern and his faculty had doubts about charter status. They worried about moving to the fringes of a public education system they all deeply believed in. They feared the potential of a divide-and-conquer strategy. The state was still a troubling unknown as a partner.

Nevertheless, life was becoming increasingly difficult under the heavy hand of New York City bureaucracy. When the faculty of International finally opted to become a charter school in the late spring of 1999, they were reacting to a large and growing list of daily frustrations, of which the following are a sample:

Student selection. Just as International was debating charter status, the NYC Board of Education's High Schools Division began insisting the school use a new computerized formula for student selection. Under the formula, the school would choose half its students and the city would assign the other half, to create a school population in which 68 percent of the students are reading at or near grade level, 16 percent are above grade level, and 16 percent below grade level. Even granting that the formula was nobly intended to assure student diversity, it was clear that International would be sent exactly the wrong kids.

International was created to serve a population that functioned well below grade level in English—mostly recent immigrants, some of whom were being introduced to the language for the first time. Nevertheless, the computer system produced for International a list of 500 students, 80 percent of whom were fluent English speakers!

International's appeal to be exempted from the computerized formula was initially rejected, as was its claim that its impending charter status granted it the right to select its own students. The school threatened to withdraw from the charter initiative before the board, for the time being, relented.

(Nadelstern and the faculty did, in fact, believe that ensuring equity is one of the few legitimate functions of the governing bodies overseeing schools. But they understood that this determination is always subtle and complex, requires wide latitude and individual consideration, and is poorly served by simplistic formulas.)

Time for staff development. Ongoing staff development and collaboration was central to International's functioning. As in a number of New York's small schools, students would be dismissed early one afternoon each week so that the staff could have an uninterrupted, several-hour time block for analyzing progress, planning, curriculum design, and joint consideration of student work. For an overextended faculty with collaboration at the heart of its work, this time block was a necessity, not a luxury. Although the practice was a deviation from regulations involving the length of the student school day and faculty meeting time, International had conducted its staff development on Wednesday afternoons for 12 years.

The High Schools Division director, avowing support, suggested to the schools following this practice that they identify themselves and apply for a permanent variance. International and Middle College, alone among their group, discreetly declined to come forward. Sure enough, the word came back from the state that the practice was not acceptable. The schools that had sponsored the appeal were forced to seek other, often less concentrated staff development activities. International, on the other hand, continued to hold its extended weekly sessions—but at a price of eternal anxiety. Nadelstern reports that, "Whenever Wednesday rolled around, I would sit there with my hands and fingers crossed and hope that nobody from the board would walk in and casually notice that none of the kids were there."

Summer budget. A venerable practice among principals of New York City schools whose faculties plan together and work with students during the summer—typical in small schools—has been to prepay the teachers before the budget closes in June. International's teachers spent considerable summer time helping students develop their portfolios to meet graduation requirements and orienting non-English speaking students. They, like many others, were paid in June for "per session" work that would be done later.

Then came increased centralization and Ed Stanczik, the school system's special investigator for weeding out mismanagement and corruption. Practices formerly winked at were now grounds for dismissal. Principals lauded in the past for manipulating the system to benefit their teachers were now more likely to be portrayed as corrupt. Small schools like International felt the clampdown most severely. Teachers would still come in August but now at their own expense, and the strain increased.

School-based staffing. International pioneered school-based staffing in New York City, working first with the United Federation of Teachers, beginning in 1987, and then with Chancellor Fernandez. On an experimental basis, the school was authorized to create a faculty personnel committee that would have the predominant voice in the hiring of new staff. Later, International's process would serve as a model for the board's "school-based option," which currently gives more than 300 schools an increased role in faculty hiring. (International also developed a comprehensive peer review process that offered colleagues extraordinary involvement in teacher evaluation.)

But again, both recentralization and the increase in the number of small schools made it harder for the board to ignore such deviations from its standard practice. There were more attempts to place teachers at International who had been excessed elsewhere. The school was thus forced to be more creative in maintaining its vacancies until they could be filled with people of its own choosing. As the charter decision approached, the school was finding it increasingly difficult to select its faculty.

Assessment. Performance-based assessment is both the very heart of International's educational program and its greatest controversy. Sophisticated standards and procedures were developed through years of painstaking effort. Students graduate only after a portfolio demonstrating completion of 10 major "performance-based assessment tasks" (e.g., a research paper, an application of the highest level of math attainment, and an oral defense of the portfolio) has been approved by a demanding teacher/student/community panel.

As standards-based reform—and concomitant high-stakes testing—reached New York City, the faculty at International believed its entire educational approach to be in jeopardy. All students would soon need to pass Regents Exams in order to graduate. And the faculty was certain that it could not do both things well: prepare limited-English students to pass the demanding Regents Exams and focus on broader, deeper preparation through challenging performance assessment. One of International's major hopes in opting for charter status was that its new "autonomy" would give it authority to decide how its students would be assessed.

The Charter Years

International's decision, in 1999, to become a charter school, along with Middle College, was widely noted in New York education circles. Two established, respected small high schools had accepted the offer of greater decision-making authority in exchange for increased accountability. Although both "decision-making authority" and "accountability" were yet to be clearly defined, and the dual relationships with city and state jurisdictions still needed working out, it was understood that they were on the verge of a new frontier in self-governance.

There was excitement at International from the outset. A principal's letter to the community expressed hope:

> We will exist outside the orbit of the Board of Ed, free from the influence of the school district's rules and regulations. Working with the faculty, parents, and the students themselves, we will now make the important instructional decisions that affect what teachers and students do in the classroom. We will decide who should work at the school, how to develop and evaluate them, and how to expend our resources in support of teachers' efforts to promote student learning.

At first, charter status at International appeared to live up to much of its promise. A board of trustees consisting primarily of teachers actually made many of the functional decisions for the school. Neither the New York City Board of Education nor the New York State Department of Education was a particularly intrusive presence. The principal did not have to contend regularly with the NYC High Schools Division, so often an irritant in the past. The school continued to thrive.

The euphoria did not last long, however. Two issues soon dominated International's charter experience. The first, and most consuming, was testing. The second—the one ultimately most responsible for International's renunciation of charter status after two years—was financing.

It turned out that, as a charter school, International was immediately subject to the Regents testing requirements. Commissioner Richard Mills firmly held the position that all New York State high school graduates must pass Regents Exams, as soon as a variance granted to alternative schools by his predecessor expired in 2001. A little more than a month before graduation that year, both International and Middle College received the news that charter school students were not covered by the variance and would have to pass the state tests in reading and writing before receiving their diplomas. Unprepared for this turn of events, International had not ordered copies of the tests, or prepared its students to take them. The compact the school had made with its students—to base graduation solely on passing courses and the rigorous performance assessments—was broken. There was anguish and outrage.

In a letter to the school, Mills went further in making his point: "Your failure to submit the order forms or to administer the examinations specified above would be a violation of the charter, warranting revocation." There were frantic appeals from International to anyone who might influence the commissioner, including Regents and politicians. They elicited a strong letter of support from former commissioner Thomas Sobol stating that the variance he had granted five years earlier guaranteed, at least through the 2000 graduation, that International could determine its own assessment and graduation criteria. Sobol wrote:

> I recognized then, as I do now, that there is more than one effective way to educate high school students, and more than one effective way to assess their progress. State officials have no monopoly on wisdom concerning the best way to teach and evaluate students. Inasmuch as the schools requesting the variance had an established record of teaching students well, I deemed it appropriate to continue their effective practices.

The appeals were futile. Mills held firm, and International gave the tests to seniors just prior to graduation. Nine did not pass and thus did not graduate with their classmates.

On the financial side, International was surprised to face an even greater challenge due to its charter status. The funding formulas they thought guaranteed a strong financial base were being adjusted: the per-student allocation would decline sharply, and staff personnel benefits in particular would suffer.

In their second year as a charter school, Nadelstern and the International faculty were already thinking of alternatives. Charter status was not offering enough benefits to outweigh the devastating consequences financial reformulation would almost certainly bring. On the other hand, the school would not consider returning to the status quo of the NYC Board of Education. They began an intensive search for a new support base—some jurisdiction where they could enjoy a high degree of both autonomy and security. There were conversations with the administration at LaGuardia Community College, which housed International; with the teachers union; with sympathetic officials within the board of education; and with assorted state and local political figures. Late in the spring, they arrived at an historic agreement with the board of education, which would enable them to surrender charter status and still function with most of the budgetary and operational autonomy it had promised. Thus it was that the Learning Zone, a special protected status long sought by its small schools (see pages 15-16 and 94-95), arrived in New York City. International and Middle College High Schools became its first members.

While amassing an impressive success record with its students, International had to fight a number of battles to maintain its autonomy and financial viability. Yet, as shown, the staff's political savvy—i.e., their knowledge of and ability to deal effectively within the system's informal structure—enabled them to overcome a significant number of challenges.

CHAPTER 9

Making Space for Innovation: Portland

GREGORY A. SMITH

The fundamental challenge facing innovative educators committed to the creation of highly effective schools lies in establishing the conditions within which good work can occur. Sometimes school districts fail to provide such conditions, instead inhibiting innovation through the enforcement of regulations aimed at eliminating risk and variability. Often it has been these restraints that have led to widespread interest in charter schools. Charter schools would be unnecessary if public educational systems were to reinvent themselves in ways that open the door to innovation at the school level.

It is no easy task for a school system to meet accountability requirements and allow for innovation, but there are places where people are beginning to move in that direction. The effort to create smaller and more autonomous schools in a number of urban districts is visible evidence of educators' search for effective alternatives to the standardization that increasingly characterizes American education. But even this well-publicized and increasingly well-funded effort to downsize schools risks being stalled by institutional practices antithetical to the exercise of choice and judgment by teachers, parents, students, and school principals.

People associated with a collection of six *special focus schools*[1] in Portland, Oregon, have been grappling with this issue over the past seven to eight years. Their efforts have led to a set of policy recommendations aimed at supporting the innovation that is more often discouraged or prohibited by urban districts. In what follows, I will describe the creation of one of the six focus schools and the alliance it formed with its sister schools in an effort to craft policies more supportive of these homegrown educational experiments.

Establishing a Special Focus School

In 1994, the Portland Public Schools were facing a severe funding crisis brought on by a property tax limitation initiative adopted a few years earlier. This, combined with the adoption of a statewide effort to equalize funding across urban and rural districts, contributed to serious budget shortfalls for what had been one of Oregon's richest school districts.[2] The result was rising class sizes, diminished administrative support staff, and a growing uneasiness among the public about the capacity of Portland's schools to deliver a quality education.

Portland's then-superintendent Jack Bierwirth and his colleagues feared the beginning of an out-migration of current students to private or suburban schools. At that time, Portland was commonly viewed as one of the few remaining urban centers with a well-functioning school district. This was due, in part, to the fact that Portland had avoided the middle-class flight to the suburbs so problematic in other U.S. cities at the close of the twentieth century. When a few groups of parents and teachers approached Bierwirth about creating small focus schools, he took the opportunity to provide more educational choices to parents who might otherwise decide to send their children to private schools, home school them, or move out of Portland altogether.

Bierwirth was himself a former alternative school teacher and principal. Indeed, a number of other central office administrators had had similar experiences, a fact that may have contributed to their willingness to consider opening the door to the creation of such schools. After the school board's adoption of policy language that allowed for the creation of parent- and teacher-initiated schools, six

---

[1]The special focus schools also are referred to simply as *focus schools*.

[2]See Smith, "Living with Oregon's Measure," 5.

new focus schools or programs were created within the next three years. The Environmental Middle School (EMS) was one of these.[3]

The Environmental Middle School

EMS began as a dream of Portland Public Schools elementary teacher Sarah Taylor. Taylor was able to bring interested teachers, parents, students, and community members together to embark on a creative journey with a shared vision. This fluid and loosely knit collection of people met to discuss and imagine the possibilities of alternatives in education that would specifically address care of the earth and also meet the needs of young adolescents in a public school setting. People shared a common interest in creating a small middle school unlike the district's large ones that had 500 to 1,000 students or more. As planning began, a particular interest emerged in serving Native American children and in approaching the curriculum with insights from Indian understandings of human-environment relationships. Not long after this group began meeting, the district offered EMS a section of a centrally located school that was experiencing declining enrollment. The school was close to public transportation, and its grounds were large enough to accommodate student gardens. So EMS began.

However, given their preoccupation with the district's financial woes, central office administrators provided little support or supervision during the school's first two years. EMS began classes with neither desks nor textbooks. But the most serious problems during this time arose from the lay off of 300 teachers, including three from EMS, in the spring of 1995, and within-district transfer policies. Public protests, coupled with a city-initiated bailout of the district, allowed the pink-slipped teachers to return for EMS's second year; some, however, decided to move elsewhere. The within-district transfer policies then assigned displaced teachers from EMS's host school to EMS, regardless of their qualifications or suitability—a situation that

[3]The others were the da Vinci Arts Middle School, WinterHaven School (accelerated learning with emphasis on math, science, technology, and character education), the Family Cooperative School (with a strong emphasis on family involvement), and the Northeast Community School (which stressed community education but closed for a variety of reasons in 1999). These five joined the Piagetian K-5 Southeast Science Learning Center, a small focus school that had already been in existence for some years.

undermined teacher collaboration and school-parent relationships for a number of years.

All of the focus schools were also constrained by the district's adherence to an initial agreement that limited their budgets to no more than the state's per-pupil funding allowance. Positions for administrative or clerical support had to be taken from this amount, a condition that led EMS to have the highest student-teacher ratio in the district for a number of years. In addition, funds for support staff such as a counselor, physical education or music teacher, or librarian were unavailable.

Despite these difficulties, the Environmental Middle School was able to establish a credible program during its first three years and attract a loyal following of students and parents. One of the reasons for its success lay in the fact that the new principal at the elementary school where EMS was housed was busy getting to know her staff and managing an unfamiliar building. This principal was also only a few years away from retirement and no longer needed to prove anything to the central office. She let EMS go its own way without interfering in its development.

When she retired during the school's third year, however, all of this changed; the new principal was also new to the district and intent on enforcing district regulations. Unlike the previous principal, he assumed day-to-day authority over the Environmental Middle School, precipitating an ongoing series of conflicts that would only be resolved with his departure from the school. This shift in leadership brought to the surface many of the frustrations that had been tolerated during the focus schools' initial start-up years and led to the formation of an alliance.

Creating an Alliance of Focus Schools

Conversations with faculty at other focus schools revealed that EMS was not alone in encountering problems with its host school, governance, insufficient resources, or within-district transfers. The situation at some of the schools had become so critical that they were considering taking advantage of a new state law sanctioning the creation of charter schools. Wanting to bring their concerns to the attention of the district and the public, teachers and parents associated with the six small focus schools organized a meeting aimed at celebrating what they had accomplished and communicating some of the district-caused difficulties that were inhibiting their development. Students, teachers, parents, and community members spoke at this meeting. Approximately 50 people were in attendance, including a central office administrator.

As a result of this gathering, the district created the Special Focus Schools Task Force. The group was charged with developing guidelines that would improve district relations with the focus schools so that parents and teachers would not be forced to utilize the charter school legislation to guarantee the continued evolution of their schools.

Working throughout the spring, the task force presented its recommendations to district administrators in late May 1999. They included statements about governance, building space, notification and enrollment, staffing, and evaluation. A number of critical concerns were raised in the task force report. Under the category of governance, the task force, among other things, indicated a need to clarify the level of autonomy focus schools possessed when they were located in a host school; stressed the importance of their active participation in the selection of faculty; and emphasized their desire to manage their own budgets, plan and implement their own staff development, and develop their own curriculum. The task force also argued that focus schools should be allowed to apply for waivers when confronted with changes in district policies not in keeping with their own unique missions, and that they should be given the opportunity to choose their own administrative structures.[4]

Although some of the small focus schools experienced amicable relations with their host schools, the task force reinforced the importance of providing facilities that were suitable and adequate for enrollment growth. In addition, members indicated that choosing buildings where administrators and teachers were willing to welcome another school was critical. Then recommendations regarding notification and enrollment called for a consistent and coordinated student recruitment and application process, as well as more effort on the part of the district to inform its constituents about the focus schools. Staffing, as mentioned in connection with the Environmental Middle

---

[4]See Special Focus Schools Task Force, "Special Focus Schools."

School, had been an especially contentious issue. The task force challenged the district practice of surplusing teachers from other schools into their programs when such individuals were unable or unwilling to incorporate the mission of the school into their teaching. It proposed that the focus schools be allowed to create school-based hiring committees and to have the opportunity to determine the best use of allocated FTE[5] and support staff.

Recognizing that their request for increased flexibility must be balanced with accountability to the district, the task force spelled out a common evaluation procedure and promised to submit annual surveys from parents, students, and faculty, as well as anecdotal records, photos, and examples of student work. Furthermore, it indicated that each focus school would provide evaluation reports conducted by "critical friends"—i.e., teams of teachers, parents, university faculty, and community members from a sister focus school. These critical friends would be responsible for making at least one site visit to a partner school over the course of the academic year. Finally, the focus schools would submit data regarding total school enrollment broken down to indicate standard demographic categories, average daily attendance, student turnover rate, student scores on standardized tests, student/teacher ratio, staffing patterns, and numbers of categorical students.

A little more than two years after the Special Focus Schools Task Force completed its work, its recommendations remained only partially acknowledged. The report was never formally considered by the school board, although a recently established committee is revisiting the question of how the district should formalize its relationship with the focus schools and developing its own policy recommendations. In the interim, the board adopted a strategic plan that emphasized the value of site-based decision making and innovation. Implementation of this plan, however, has been erratic. Following the removal of the superintendent who spurred the plan's creation, its future has become uncertain.

Yet, conversations begun with central office administrators during the task force meetings did result in positive movement. Some, but not all, of the special focus schools now have more authority over hiring

[5]Full-time equivalent (FTE)

decisions. In addition, more flexible administrative arrangements have been adopted in some schools. In the summer of 1999, following the meetings of the task force, the founder and coordinator of the Environmental Middle School was granted the status of administrative assistant. Rather than reporting to the host school's principal, she reports to her district-level supervisor. And in the spring of 2001, the school board made EMS a "pilot school," a new designation that reclassified the school's coordinator as a part-time principal and provided funds for a secretary. This move freed money to hire more teachers. But with the exception of the da Vinci Arts Middle School, which has more than 300 students and is classified as a school rather than a program, the remaining special focus schools retain their status as programs within host schools. As before, this status is workable for some and problematic for others.

By far the greatest challenge now facing the special focus schools is one that was not anticipated by the task force. One of the results of the districtwide strategic plan has been the devolution of some decision-making power from the central office to neighborhood schools. Teachers and parents can now participate in conversations about whether or not they wish to continue hosting a special focus school. In the case of the Environmental Middle School, teachers and parents at the host neighborhood school—an elementary school—have discussed the possibility of extending and becoming a K-8 school, in an effort to attract enough students to keep the building open if EMS were to move or close. Nothing as yet has come of those discussions, but the process of working through such issues has been stressful for people in both schools.

Looking to the Future

Current developments underscore the importance of establishing clear policies at the district level to support the creation and sustenance of small, special focus schools. In Portland, a brief opening of the administrative gates that either sanction or deny educational innovation allowed teachers and parents to take the lead in developing what have been, in effect, within-district charter schools. Those gates remained open for only a short time, however, and the district has struggled to accommodate these atypical schools ever since. The work of the Special Focus Schools Task Force identified ways to overcome some of these difficulties. If adopted, their recommendations might free the special focus schools from the need to live from one crisis to another.

Meanwhile, since the fall of 2000, the successful pursuit of grants by the Portland Public School District and the Portland Schools Foundation to create small learning communities in district high schools has brought the value of smaller schools and site-based innovation to the forefront of many peoples' minds. And since this is a district effort, central administration may be more receptive to addressing the issues with which the focus schools have wrestled. It is possible this initiative may result in policy changes that more actively encourage the kinds of educational experiments and practices encountered in the special focus schools.

CHAPTER 10

A Multiplex: The Julia Richman Education Complex

The search for hospitable physical environments has been a particular preoccupation of small schools. Schools that have their own space from the beginning are generally the most envied. However, the spectrum of these accommodations ranges from new buildings built specifically for the school—the rare lucky ones—to deteriorating storefronts. Small schools sometimes find a separate space within a commercial building or one housing other governmental agencies. In many of these cases, educational facilities are lacking (e.g., gymnasia, performance spaces, labs) and the tensions of adapting to the needs of workers and/or the public sharing the building are often overwhelming.

The majority of small schools find themselves housed in larger schools. Sometimes they reside in the larger schools from which they were derived, as special programs granted some autonomy. Often they are brought into "host" buildings as separate entities and are expected to accommodate the sometimes highly disparate cultures of the school or schools surrounding them. Competition, resource limitations, and, often, outright hostility are the all-too-common products of such arrangements. It is these schools that are in particular need of creative, supportive policy structures that protect their autonomy and maintain their resources.

The Julia Richman High School campus in New York City became the focus of one of the most innovative and closely watched attempts to create desirable housing arrangements for small schools. Julia Richman was one of two large, failing high schools designated for restructuring under the Coalition Campus Project (CCP) in the early 1990s; of the two, Julia Richman's restructuring effort was the most successful. The Center for Collaborative Education (with Deborah Meier at the helm), the city, and the teachers union agreed to create six new small schools to serve the population of Julia Richman. The school would phase out its current student enrollment in three years, then reopen as a new complex of small schools. Meanwhile the new schools would begin life in separate "hothouse" spaces until the newly reconfigured Julia Richman Education Complex was ready to accommodate them.

The six schools were designed using the principles of the Coalition of Essential Schools and were successfully launched. Only two of the schools, however, actually moved as originally planned into the Julia Richman building, though all continue to thrive today in various spaces. As it happened, the Julia Richman Education Complex brought in two additional small high schools (one an arts program that had been part of the original Julia Richman), a preK-8 elementary school, and a special middle school for autistic students. The complex also incorporated a variety of service agencies within the building, including a medical center, day care facility, arts center, and teacher professional development center. The range of schools and services were part of a deliberate design to build a comprehensive, inclusive, diverse community.

The CCP fought to bring the school primarily under the jurisdiction of the alternative schools superintendency to provide some insulation from traditional board of education requirements.[1] They struggled to be allowed to make Julia Richman a multiage facility, and when the Ella Baker Elementary School joined the complex through a

[1]One school in the building, Talent Unlimited, does report to the Manhatten high schools superintendent and another, P226M, reports to the special education superintendent.

special arrangement, it became the first elementary school to be accepted into the alternative schools superintendency. The CCP was explicit that each school in the complex must be considered an "autonomous unit having control over curriculum, educational philosophy, staffing pattern, schedule, and organization."[2] They also knew, at the same time, that they needed to create a governance structure that would assure harmony and collaboration among schools and some sense of overall community.

It is the Julia Richman Governing Council that, probably more than any other organizational feature, sets the school apart.[3] The governing council is composed of the principals and directors of each of the small schools, plus the program heads. "Eight or 10 distinct voices are regularly heard," says a participant. Meetings are weekly, often long, and attendance is held sacrosanct.

The council's charge is extensive. On the broadest level is the task of balancing the schools' needs for individual autonomy and self definition with the need to coexist harmoniously in shared space. The council provides a forum for all the schools to articulate their particular needs and concerns, while simultaneously developing a unified voice to lend weight to their dealings with the outside world. On the concrete level, there is common space to be constantly negotiated, there is collective safety to be carefully watched, and there are joint personnel and budgetary decisions to be shared. Sometimes the personnel/budget decisions can be tough ones. For example, when the district assigned a technology person to the complex whom the directors and principals did not find acceptable, they collectively refused to accept that person's assignment, even though it wound up costing them the position. They have since gone without a dedicated technologist but maintain that they have never regretted their decision.

The Julia Richman Complex may not be unique in having its component schools represented in a governance body, but it is distinguished by the fervent commitment of each of its schools to the process. Decisions are made by consensus, which often adds time and

---

[2]In Cook, "The Transformation of One Large Urban High School," 108.

[3]This group was formerly called the building council, then renamed to reflect its weighty charge. But, according to one of the participants, the new name "makes some of the authorities nervous because it implies that we govern ourselves."

energy to the deliberations but is an integral symbol of the group's egalitarian spirit. The commitment to dealing collectively with issues that in other buildings would more than likely fall to a single decision maker guarantees greater openness and confidence in the fairness of the process. "We're equal partners here," said Lucy Matos, the former principal of Ella Baker Elementary, of the governing council. "We function as a single interrelated unit. We're the policymakers, decision makers, operations managers. Our formula is to have found like-minded people who say, 'Let's reconfigure space, time, money, and be clear about locating responsibility.'"

The players in the Julia Richman Governing Council have not always been "like-minded." The principal of Talent Unlimited, who was an administrator at Julia Richman before the reorganization, found himself explaining his more traditional school to his new "alternative" colleagues. The principal of at least one of the schools had originally had his mind set on being in his own building. In addition, secondary and elementary schools have potentially conflicting needs, as do regular and special education programs. There are also contrasting personalities and styles at the table. What, then, makes this particular process functional?

It undoubtedly helps that the principals and directors fundamentally respect and, from all accounts, like each other. But Jacqueline Ancess identifies organizational features that also contribute to their success:

> Although the schools belong to three superintendencies, they are unified in their commitment to self-governance and building accountability, they brook no external interference, they guard their autonomy, and they risk fighting Board of Ed policies that they feel are not in the best interests of their students, school, and the building.[4]

She points out that their dedication to "the dialectic between autonomy and community helps schools stay focused on their raison d'etre: the education of their students."[5] She maintains that both their

---

[4]In Ancess and Ort, *How the Coalition Campus Schools Have Reimagined High School,* 69.

[5]Ibid., 56.

commitment to and capacity to tolerate diversity are critical, as is their capacity to compromise.[6] The invariable weekly meetings and obligatory attendance are important, as is the culture that brings delicate issues regularly to the table, rather than dealing with them in back offices or unilaterally.

Internal cohesion is not the only benefit of an effective governing council. Small schools with limited power bases benefit greatly from speaking as part of a larger unit, and a unified voice in dealing with the board of education has become a fundamental principle at Julia Richman. "Our approach to the superintendencies is keeping them at a respectful distance," said Matos. "Sometimes we need to communicate with them individually, of course. But whenever anything affects the building, we respond as one voice. We make sure never, ever to respond as a split team."

There is one other major feature contributing to the Julia Richman Complex's successful self-management. The complex's building manager coordinates the schools' efforts, brings them together, facilitates the governing council, and manages the daily business that cuts across all schools. By design, there is no schoolwide principal; rather, the building manager is a peer who works in easy collaboration with the small schools' leaders. From the beginning, the building manager at Julia Richman has been Herb Mack, a codirector of the Urban Academy, one of the small schools located in the complex. The schools were offered an assistant principal position but declined in favor of retaining the building manager role. The building manager supervises the maintenance and security staffs, schedules common spaces, and coordinates relationships with the community and outside agencies. A key to Mack's success in the role, his colleagues say, is his nonauthoritarian stance and his view of himself as a supporter, facilitator, and peer.

Small schools looking to find congenial environments in which to function would do well to study the Julia Richman model. Ann Cook, also a codirector of the Urban Academy, sees four factors as critical to success: school autonomy, with each school coming to the collaboration as an equal partner; building management by consensus decision making; system support, with commitment from the central board on

---

[6]Ibid., 70-72.

basic principles of redesign; and small schools, with the opportunity to create community for both students and teachers.

> The transformation of Julia Richman High School into an educational complex is a story worth telling. Turning a school around—one that only five years ago saw fewer than 10% of its students finish high school—and replacing it with schools that graduate almost 90% of their entering students is certainly major news. So too is the transformation of a building where security scanners once occupied center stage to a complex where safety, without metal detectors, is now taken for granted by students, teachers, and neighborhood residents as well as by parents whose small children attend the early childhood classes in the elementary school.[7]

Of course, the schools continue to encounter challenges posed by the larger system (most recently in the form of the Regents tests all New York high school students must take). But, due to the way in which the schools of the Julia Richman Complex have chosen to govern themselves, building governance has not been a source of difficulty.

[7]In Cook, *The Transformation of One Large Urban High School,* 117-118.

Chapter 11

Conclusions

The observations reported here have reconfirmed some of our prior convictions, challenged some, and added a few more. Perhaps the most fundamental is an observation that has become almost commonplace to make: successful, enduring change and reform in schools requires change and reform at the system level.

But rarely is it stated just what sort of change is required. As succeeding pages show, small schools are a major case in point. Indeed, if the widely sought smaller learning communities are to thrive and to last, along with the reforms we hope they will generate, then either a virtually whole new set of policies must be written at the system level or a new flexibility quite foreign to bureaucracy must permeate all existing policy. The only other option is a radical devolution of authority over schools. We can no longer continue to say that we want improvement—and the change and new institutions that must entail—while continuing to insist on the practices and procedures we now require of all schools. These practices and procedures may be exactly what must be changed to permit improvement. As others have said, you can't keep doing what you have been doing—even if harder or longer or with more determination—and hope for very different results than you have been getting. So, if schools are to change much for the better, there must be changes in the way they go about their business. This, in turn, means that there must be changes in the rules that govern them and in the systems that manage them. Most of the conclusions that follow address system-imposed difficulties that small schools and schools-within-schools face, but a few contain suggestions for what these programs might do to try to deal with these difficulties.

Changes in rules. In the school systems we studied, we did not see much evidence anywhere of this sort of change. Instead, we observed attempts to accommodate new and very different sorts of organizational units by granting waivers and exemptions. This strategy may be useful for a trial period, to help decide whether an innovation is worth keeping, but even then it biases the test in favor of the status quo and against the changes for which advocates of innovation seek the exemptions. It does so in at least five ways:

First, the granting of waivers—or the withholding of them—is frequently arbitrary and capricious. These decisions are often made on a case-by-case basis by persons whose primary responsibility is to monitor conformance; thus, they are often, and quite understandably, unwilling to declare a rule or regulation unnecessary. And even if the willingness is there, "whenever they look at a problem," as Deborah Meier put it, "they've been trained to seek, first and foremost, ways to solve it by rule. If it's not good for everyone, it's not good for anyone. To make exceptions smacks of favoritism and inefficiency. Each exception thus must be defended over and over again."[1]

Second, the need to request repeated exemptions puts the small schools at a significant disadvantage. It is almost inevitable that they come to be perceived within the system as "precious" institutions that, a bit like spoiled children, are constantly demanding special attention and consideration.

Third, policy by exception is sometimes a way to get around mandates and taboos, but it is unlikely to permit much in the way of positive support, which is widely recognized as vital to the success of reform efforts. In locales where resources are not plentiful, exemption from regulations is a different matter from providing extra resources, though small schools often require both. The former may be a matter

[1]In Meier, "Can the Odds Be Changed?" 186.

of rule bending, but the latter is often taken as a direct violation of the demands of equity.

Fourth, policy by exception may be feasible for dealing with an innovation that is relatively simple and not widely adopted. But when an innovation is as multifaceted as small schools (involving curriculum, school organization, activities, etc.) and involves a number of schools, it puts tremendous strains on the system. As an aide to one of New York's deputy chancellors put it, "For every aspect of this someone has to spend time and energy finding a way through the regulations, to let whatever happens happen without being entirely out of compliance."[2]

And fifth, as outcomes one through four suggest, policy by exemption keeps the system intact and unreformed. It makes it unnecessary for the system to examine the way it operates with respect to all schools. It thus makes it less likely that the system will, in Ms. Rizzo's terms (see page 7), be able to accommodate more than one organizational model.

The most difficult rule. As preceding pages show, the single practice that is perhaps most inimical to the success of small schools and schools-within-schools is what is usually a teachers' union contract provision: the right of teachers to fill openings based on their seniority within the system. Small schools and schools-within-schools are typically based on a like-minded faculty, and often one that has undergone a particular sort of professional development together. When new teachers are brought in who know nothing of the theme or focus of the program and who, in fact, may be quite indifferent or even unsympathetic to it, not only is the program's effectiveness severly underminded, but its faculty's morale may suffer intensely. Uninformed or hostile newcomers have been known to destroy programs.

In acknowledgement of this, New York City's United Federation of Teachers agreed to an arrangement that is now a regular provision within the contract: when 75 percent of a school's or school-within-a-school's teachers agree, seniority transfer rights are suspended, and instead, a personnel committee, which in-

[2]In Darling-Hammond et al., "Inching toward Reform in New York City," 174. Recall the statement made by Phillips, New York's alternative schools superintendent, that he spent half his time trying to find ways around the rules.

cludes teachers, selects new hires. Recently, the percent of agreement necessary was reduced to 50.

Active support or leadership. It appears that for a major reform to succeed, more than the mere approval of the person at the top is required. Without this person's active and enthusiastic support, it may be possible to get major reform such as school downsizing going, but it is awfully hard to sustain it. (As an example, though institutionalization of the SWSs framework at Kapaa Elementary School is more than a decade old and firmly set in place, it remains uncertain how long the arrangement can outlive Cliff Bailey, the principal who installed and nurtured it so carefully.)

Line office with responsibility for oversight. Because of the multiple functions of a superintendent or CEO, in educational systems (as opposed to single schools) that are seeking major change, it also helps to have an office highly placed within the administrative structure that is charged solely with nurturing, sustaining, and advocating for the change. Placing such responsibility in the hands of an assistant to a high official will not suffice. It must be a line office with responsibility for the oversight of the new schools. And even this arrangement may not suffice, particularly when change occurs at the top, as the story of New York's alternative schools superintendency suggests; but it seems a highly important aid to success.

Use of informal systems. Though bureaucracies are always governed by rules, there are still "informal" systems operating in each one. There are some individuals who are more likely to say yes than others and some infractions that are more likely to be winked at. There are friendships, informal networks, and opportunities that arise due to circumstances and relationships. The stories told by Stephen Phillips, the former superintendent of alternative schools in New York, of how the Boys Choir of Harlem became the New York Family Academy, and of how the move to terminate the alternative schools superintendency was averted, are clear illustrations of this. Even with his authority as a superintendent, Phillips relied at least as often on the informal system as the formal one. At Kapaa Elementary School, principal Cliff Bailey also became a master navigator of the informal systems operating within the state, obtaining funds and remaining a successful maverick for the reform path he chose. The political savvy displayed by the staff at International High School in New York City exemplified its ability to maneuver within the informal system. Particularly for small schools or schools-within-schools lacking formal support, it could be a great help to learn how to operate effectively within the informal system.

The creation of alliances. At least until the sorts of system changes recommended here have been adopted, it might well be wise for small schools and schools-within-schools to seek alliances with other such programs within their districts. If there are opportunities to form the sort of alliance that involves like-minded or similarly oriented programs, this affords opportunities for networking and collaboration that can yield much by way of professional development and organizational learning for the schools involved. This is the kind of connection New York's Coalition schools have enjoyed. But even where this is not the case—as in Boston's Pilot schools, Portland's focus schools, and even Julia Richman's programs—it has been politically useful to get together in dealing with the district and to speak with a single voice. It can also help those belonging to such an alliance to deal with some of the widespread problems pointed out in this chapter.

Adverse effects of top leadership change. Change in top leadership may well prove inimical to school reform. That may sound strange, since we frequently change leaders precisely in the interest of positive change and improvement. But the frequency with which this happens in city superintendencies—the average term is now four years—makes it counter to teachers' self-preservation to invest the energy and effort major change requires in any particular superintendent's reform venture. Before the venture can be fully realized, the leader is out and replaced by a new one. And because superintendents are hired as persons of vision, each newcomer must have his or her own vision to supplant that of the predecessor. Unless they are insiders hired explicitly to sustain the preceding vision, they are expected to arrive equipped with their own. This means that schools and teachers are likely to be asked to embark on a new and different reform direction every time there is a new superintendent.

Essentially the same thing may occur with principals in many locales. In Hawaii, where principals have seniority transfer rights and salaries are tied to enrollments, some schools have frequent changes in principalship. One school is said to have had 21 principals in a period of 19 years. Principals, too, often arrive with visions, or at least convictions about what are the best school arrangements and classroom practices. Under such unstable circumstances, it is not surprising that many teachers greet a new principal with a "This, too, shall pass" attitude. The belief that this sort of turnover is inevitable is highly inimical to the major efforts teachers must invest in a major reform venture. (This is surely one of the reasons why Cliff Bailey's teachers were so reluctant to step forward and why he promised them early on that he would remain at Kapaa for at least three years.)

To address this barrier to school improvement and reform, school districts might well offer teachers investing time and effort in major reform efforts some sort of guarantee—perhaps in the form of a compact, if not a contract—that the reform venture will endure for a reasonable minimal period, or that they will have a voice in its discontinuance. (The latter is to cover the possibility that a reform effort may not work and may have to be discontinued right away.) This would restrict the authority of new administrations (be it a superintendent or, within a school, a principal) to wipe the slate clean. And while it is conceivable that in some instances this would be unfortunate, an up-front guarantee of some sort may be the only way to keep teachers from becoming so cynical that they are simply unwilling to cooperate in school improvement efforts.

Demands for school accountability. We feel that, ultimately, the fate of the small schools movement may rest on just how today's pervasive demands for school accountability and standards are carried out. The jury is still out on just what the nature of the standards should be. On the one hand are those who see the standards movement as a means of controlling the curriculum and its organization in considerable detail in all schools. On the other are those who seek only to assure that students have acquired important concepts and common understandings, as well as intellectual skills and abilities. The second interpretation leaves room for considerable innovation as to curriculum and its presentation. The first leaves room for very little, which is not universally viewed as a disadvantage and is precisely the appeal of standards to many. Yet, the success of the small schools movement is contingent upon the triumph of the second interpretation.

A lot will also depend on the nature of the tests required by the new federal law, information that has not yet been revealed in many states. (Since the new legislation requires annual testing in grades 3 through 8, few, if any, states at this point have selected or designed all of the tests they will use.) If the tests emphasize intellectual skills, such as analysis, inference drawing, separating fact from interpretation, and judgment, then students dealing with nontraditional curriculum—or traditional curriculum in nontraditional ways—should have no more difficulty than students from conventional schools. Few small schools advocates could oppose such tests. If the content questions address concepts instead of fact retention, again there should be no difficulty or opposition. For instance, a question and directive may be posed to students this way: What are the causes of war? Apply your generalizations by examining one war in detail and citing the specifics leading up to it. Such questions are far less curriculum biased than questions about the antagonists involved in the Boxer Rebellion or about two particular Civil War generals and their accomplishments.

So, the way in which the standards movement, with its required tests, is played out may go a long way in determining whether the most innovative of the small schools can survive or, indeed, whether innovation of any sort can be admitted.

Federal requirements for research-based school reform. Another factor that remains uncertain at the moment but will play a part in determining whether the new small schools can survive is the extent to which comprehensive school reform and the Obey-Porter variety of legislation come to dominate state and federal grant making to schools. While this approach to school improvement insists on the multifaceted reform plan that small schools advocates also insist on, it restricts support only to innovations that have amassed a positive research record. Unless you want to do something that others have already done and that has been acceptably researched, you will receive no support for it.

This requirement is directly at odds with the many small school advocates who insist that programs be designed by the teachers who will operate them. At this point, a slight bit of wiggle room remains. For example, one of the approved comprehensive school reform models that is perhaps less favored than the more structured and explicit ones, is the Coalition of Essential Schools model. It has been used extensively among New York's small schools, permitting schools that look quite different from one another as to theme, staffing, and curricular and instructional approaches. But unless a new venture is disposed to the progressive orientation of the Coalition of Essential Schools, the permissible choices for Obey-Porter-type funding may well prove quite constraining.

Protection from bureaucratic pressures to conform. As long as schools remain units within bureaucracies, some structural arrangements must protect the innovative ones from the normal bureaucratic pressures pushing them to be identical to other units. Without such arrangements, as preceding pages show, an innovative school is under constant pressure to become like other schools, i.e., to drop the very arrangements and practices that make it a reform. One way that has been devised to accomplish this is to establish a special district or set of schools that are governed and authorized to behave differently than other schools in the same jurisdiction.

Perhaps the best model yet to emerge for such arrangements is Deborah Meier's conception of a *Learning Zone*, which she proposed for New York City. It would place similarly minded schools (i.e., schools sharing a single philosophy and/or approach) within a single Learning Zone, irrespective of their geographic proximity to one another. The zone would set up its own expectations and the schools within it would be responsible to one another for fulfilling them. Although the model does not suggest that the state would have no authority over Learning Zone schools, it does suggest that the district—the City of New York—would have little remaining authority over them.

Another model has been developed by David Ericson at the University of Hawaii.[3] He proposes dividing all schools into complexes consisting of a high school, plus the elementary and junior high (or middle) schools from which its students come. In Ericson's model, a complex would not be responsible to state authorities. The governing group of a complex would consist of community members and professional staff, and its authority over the schools would be complete and final, so long, of course, as it did not violate the constitution, federal law, or health and safety laws.

New York's former chancellor Harold Levy adopted another conception of a Learning Zone and put it into operation. (See chapter 8 for an account of one of its two initial members and how that school came to enjoy this protected status.) The zone is, in effect, an in-district

---

[3]See Ericson, "Just Who Rules the Schools in Hawaii—And Who Should?"

charter arrangement that gives members both the same sorts of freedoms Boston's Pilot schools are supposed to enjoy (see chapter 6) and a place in the system; it creates a unit that separates and frees them from the mandates and prohibitions that apply to other units.

The Learning Zone was to be created by the system in cooperation with the teachers and administrators unions. Its schools have the "regulatory and contractual autonomy available to charter schools" and in exchange are to assume "increased responsibility and accountability for student achievement."[4] The zone's seven-member board of directors consists of the chancellor, the two union presidents, and other leaders outside the schools. The zone reports to the deputy chancellor for instruction, who is advised by a zone coordinating council consisting of each zone school's principal, teachers union leader, and parent association president, plus ex officio union and board of education representatives. This group is chaired by a principal of one of the zone schools.

Each school has a school advisory committee composed of parents, teachers, administrators, and other staff, and elected by their own constituencies. This group reviews the budget, staffing, and instructional plans; assesses student performance; and develops plans for improving it. Members also determine school and class size within budget allocations. Learning Zone schools receive full per-student funding from local, state, and federal sources, and they determine their own budgetary allocations. They handle their own purchasing. A personnel committee that includes teachers, administrators, parents, and students establishes criteria and qualifications for open positions, and "the most senior applicant will be selected among *qualified* individuals."[5]

According to the Learning Zone plan, teachers are guaranteed a minimum of a two-hour time block weekly, within the school day, to work collaboratively. Within broad frameworks, they design their own instructional program, activities, schedule, and assessments. Accountability is "for student performance outcomes and not the process by which they are attained."[6]

---

[4]In Levy, 1.

[5]Levy, 1, emphasis in the original.

[6]Levy, 3.

Rethinking the principalship. A penultimate conclusion we have reached is that perhaps we ought to reexamine current ideas about the principalship. A number of people have begun asking whether we have expected too much of principals. We ask them to be leaders and managers and, in some respects, function as CEOs; in other respects we ask them to act like middle managers. Some feel we have created a job impossible for anyone to do; others feel we have created position holders who block as often as they foster school improvement.

Whether it is because of an innate human need or because bureaucracies create insecurities in middle managers, there is no question that individuals' acquisition and retention of administrative power and control is an issue in our schools. In government, the solution to this challenge is the division of power, so that no branch of government controls it all. In both government and education, we have recognized—and criticized intensely—the tendency for the central figures in a bureaucratic system to gather and concentrate power in their own hands. In educational systems, the proper antidote to such tendencies has been the diffusion of power to individual schools. So, the last 10 or 15 years of school reform have witnessed a call for the return of decision-making authority to the schools from central offices. What we have seen much less of, however, is a concern with the concentration of power in the hands of principals. The concept of shared decision making is linked occasionally to the idea of school-based management, but in practice, this idea rarely gets past a rhetorical mention.

In a way, our overlooking of the likely consequences of decentralization is strange: exactly the same principles govern the need to diffuse authority within a school as the need to diffuse it within a school system. Fewer attempts have been made to deal with the system's downloaded authority to principals beyond expression of concern about overburdening them. And, indeed, very little concern about this seems to have been expressed.

In fact, almost the reverse has occurred. Considerable reform literature, especially that still emanating from the Effective Schools movement, has sought to strengthen the principalship, i.e., expand the principal's role, authority, and control. We have done this to such an extent that there are now cries that we are expecting and demanding too much of principals, and that we have stretched their responsibilities too far. As one recent study pointed out, particularly in poorly performing schools, "the heroic model of urban principalship has run its course and may even be dysfunctional."[7] Among principals themselves, there are complaints that new responsibilities have been added while control has been diminished, for example, by school advisory councils, shared decision making requirements, or by a reduction in curricular choices resulting from the standards movement. But principals nevertheless retain what amounts in many places to dictatorial powers with respect to teachers. And they are very much concerned with power and control. A recent study of what administrative interns are taught by their mentors revealed the extent to which such professional preparation emphasizes the centrality of control and status awareness to fledgling school administrators.[8]

Perhaps the time has come for us to look to other in-school governance arrangements. It is a difficult matter because the importance of leadership has been so strongly emphasized for years. And there can be little doubt that in many schools, strong leadership is much needed. It is also clear that teachers within a school often have little understanding of—and, under present conditions, scant interest in—schoolwide considerations. This is patent in the attitudes of teachers in a number of miserably failing schools, who see the need for no more than Bandaids—a bit of curricular tinkering and possibly a couple of staff changes. There are also places where teachers have been so infantalized over a period of years that they have become highly dependent upon a leader to direct and control their performance. This can sometimes lead to a codependency situation wherein those who are drawn to the principalship want to dominate, and teachers want to be told what to do.

It is a difficult question. As one politically sophisticated teacher (an ex-lawyer) mused a decade ago, "What's really needed is a principal with unlimited power who is a total democrat by conviction and inclination." He was fortunate enough to be teaching in a small school where that seemed to be the case. It is a situation that is difficult to find though, and certainly not one we can attempt to

---

[7]In Payne and Kaba, "So Much Reform, So Little Change," 16.

[8]See Fishbein and Osterman, "Crossing Over."

replicate with much confidence. (Indeed, we tried during the '50s, when there was much talk among administrators and in administrator-preparation materials about "democratizing" school administration.) But since the challenge and need are both intense and important, at least three possible remedies occur to us.

In small schools or SWSs, where the teachers are ready (read "willing") to take it on, let there be teacher leaders who manage and lead, even though this may require some changes in certification requirements. A codirectorship, or troika-type of leadership arrangement, has been undertaken in some schools where teachers with somewhat reduced teaching loads divide the functions among them. Another arrangement that has met with success is the election of a leader by staff for a three- or four-year term. Schools or SWSs beginning this way may or may not choose to retain the arrangement (see, for example, Deborah Meier's account of how she evolved from a teacher leader to a principal at Central Park East Elementary School); but at least they will have had the opportunity to try it.

In a system that has restructured, i.e., turned to small, diversified SWSs, a variation of an arrangement operating in Toronto some years ago might be a good idea. There, a principal was assigned responsibility for four or five schools-within-schools existing in various buildings. We are facing a national shortage of principals anyway. Why not let the SWSs operate under the supervision of itinerant principals, each of whom is responsible for a set of three to five SWSs (operating in different buildings) that share an educational orientation among themselves and with the principal? Teacher leadership would have to emerge in the absence of a full-time, on-site principal, and the principal would have to allocate his or her time as needed. For example, the principal might take up residence for weeks at a time in a SWAS that was in trouble, then in smoother times, spend a full day each week at each one. Such an arrangement might not only address the authority problem but also the challenge of teacher commitment and professionalization, both of which appear linked to cultivating a wider concern with, and responsibility for, the improvement of the total endeavor, the whole school.

In schools not ready or willing to try the teacher leader or itinerant principal strategies, a third, two-step process may be applicable. First, schools should be held publicly accountable not only for student achievement but also for the things for which principals are more directly responsible. These include establishing arrangements (structures, policies, procedures) that actually support teaching and learning, positive school climates, and sound and appropriate professional development opportunities. Second, each school's teachers and parents, and perhaps students as well, should be surveyed periodically—say, every two years—on these matters. After four years, a principal's potential reappointment to a particular school would be based in considerable part on the results of these surveys, plus related records (e.g., teacher attendance and retention rates). Principals of buildings where there are SWSs should be held responsible for the extent to which they have helped the SWSs to develop their own themes and climates, and given the SWSs moral and other support and the freedom to operate their programs. Superordinates may wish to consider other matters as well in making the reappointment decision, but surely these key responsibilities should weigh heavily—at least as heavily as test scores—in determining whether a principal is doing the job adequately. Otherwise, it may be hard to tell why a school's performance is not improving and who is responsible.

There are principals who would object sorely to these suggestions. It would be important to learn whether those who do are operating on a zero-sum conception of power, wherein the gain of authority on the part of teachers represents a loss of their own power. If, instead, their conception of power relates to the ability to affect outcomes—i.e., success in teaching, learning, and the school's ability to influence its students—the kind of redistribution of authority within schools described here might well significantly increase the power and influence of principals. These, then, are some conclusions we feel are confirmed by the observations reported in these pages. It would be a mistake, however, to conclude without also noting one final conviction: the need for the system changes these stories suggest does not indicate that small schools and schools-within-schools are an especially "precious" or fragile reform. We are convinced that significant change of any sort must entail system change if it is to take hold and endure. Even under ideal conditions, educational change is difficult to introduce and hard to sustain. Unless all parts of the system into which it is introduced are geared toward welcoming and nurturing it, the reform will continue to prove elusive.

Bibliography

Ancess, Jacquelin, and Suzanna Wichterle Ort. *How the Coalition Campus Schools Have Reimagined High School: Seven Years Later.* New York: National Center for Restructuring Education, Schools, and Teaching, 1999.

Azcoitia, Carlos. *Report and Recommendations on Small Schools in Chicago.* Chicago: The Small Schools Task Force, 1995.

Boston Public Schools. *Focus on Children: A Comprehensive Reform Plan for the Boston Public Schools.* Boston: Boston Public Schools, 1996. ERIC Document Reproduction Service No. ED408393.

Boston Plan for Excellence in the Public Schools. *Fact Sheet: What the Boston Plan Does, 1999-2000.* Boston: Boston Plan for Excellence in the Public Schools, 2001.

Bredeson, P. V., M. J. Fruth, and K. L. Kasten. "Organizational Incentives and Secondary School Teaching." *Journal of Research and Development in Education* 16, no. 4 (1983): 52-58.

Center for Collaborative Education. *Executive Summaries of CCE Reports on the Boston Pilot Schools Network.* Boston: Center for Collaborative Education, 2001. http://ccebos.org/bsc_exec_summ_final.pdf (20 December 2002).

Center for Collaborative Education. *How Boston Pilot Schools Use Freedom Over Budget, Staffing, and Scheduling to Meet Student Needs.* Boston: Center for Collaborative Education, 2001. http://ccebos.org/pilot_resource_study_011015.pdf (20 December 2002).

Christman, Jolley Bruce. *Guidance for School Improvement in a Decentralizing System: How Much, What Kind, and from Where? Children Achieving: Philadelphia's Education Reform,* Progress Report Series 1996-1997. Philadelphia: Consortium for Policy Research in Education, Graduate School of Education, University of Pennsylvania, 1998. ERIC Document Reproduction Service No. ED423339.

Cook, Ann. "The Transformation of One Large Urban High School: The Julia Richman Education Complex." In *Creating New Schools: How Small Schools Are Changing American Education,* edited by Evans Clinchy, 101-118. New York: Teachers College Press, 2000.

Cotton, Kathleen. *Affective and Social Benefits of Small-Scale Schooling. ERIC Digest.* Charleston, WV: ERIC Clearinghouse on Rural Education and Small Schools, 1996.

Darling-Hammond, Linda, Jacqueline Ancess, Kemly McGregor, and David Zuckerman. "Inching toward Reform in New York City: The Coalition Campus Schools Project." In *Creating New Schools: How Small Schools Are Changing American Education,* edited by Evans Clinchy, 163-180. New York: Teachers College Press, 2000.

Darling-Hammond, Linda, Jacqueline Ancess, and Suzanna Wichterle Ort. "Reinventing High School: The Coalition Campus Schools Project." *American Educational Research Journal* 39, no. 3 (fall 2002): 639-673.

Domanico, Raymond. "A Small Footprint on the Nation's Largest School System." In *Can Philanthropy Fix Our Schools? Appraising Walter Annenberg's $500 Million Gift to Public Education*, 5-18. Washington, DC: The Thomas B. Fordham Foundation, 2000. ERIC Document Reproduction Service No. ED442803.

Ericson, David. "Just Who Rules the Schools in Hawaii—And Who Should?" A report to the Hawaii Educational Policy Center, University of Hawaii at Manoa, HI, December 2000.

Fetler, Mark. "School Dropout Rates, Academic Performance, Size, and Poverty: Correlates of Educational Reform," *Educational Evaluation and Policy Analysis* 11, no. 2 (1989): 109-116.

Fishbein, Susan, and Karen Osterman. "Crossing Over: Learning the Roles and Rules of the Teacher-Administrator Relationship." Paper presented at the annual meeting of the American Educational Research Association, Seattle, WA, April 2001. ERIC Document Reproduction Service No. ED463276.

Gewertz, Catherine. "It's Official: State Takes Over Philadelphia Schools." *Education Week* 21, no. 16 (2002): 1, 14-15.

Hartocollis, Anemona. "Small Schools Face Limits on Autonomy." *New York Times*, 13 October 1997, B1.

Howley, Craig, and Robert Bickel. "The Influence of Scale." *American School Board Journal* 189, no. 3 (March 2002): 28-30.

Innerst, Carol. "Grant Brings High Hopes, Modest Gains to Philadelphia School Reform." In *Can Philanthropy Fix Our Schools? Appraising Walter Annenberg's $500 Million Gift to Public Education*, 19-32. Washington, DC: The Thomas B. Fordham Foundation, 2000.

Johnston, Robert C. "Settlement Averts School Shutdown in Philadelphia." *Education Week* 19, no. 39 (2000): 3.

Katz, Michael B., Michelle Fine, and Elaine Simon. "Poking Around: Outsiders View Chicago School Reform." *Teachers College Record* 99, no. 1 (1997): 117-157.

Klonsky, Michael. "Small Schools: Creating a Model for School Restructuring in Chicago." Doctoral dissertation, University of Illinois–Chicago, 1997.

Lee, Valerie E., and Susanna Loeb. "School Size in Chicago Elementary Schools: Effects on Teachers' Attitudes and Students' Achievement." *American Educational Research Journal* 37, no. 1 (2000): 3-31.

Lee, Valerie E., and Julia B. Smith. "Effects of High School Restructuring and Size on Early Gains in Achievement and Engagement." *Sociology of Education* 68, no. 4 (1995): 241-270.

Levy, Harold O. Letter to Cecilia L. Cunningham, principal, Middle College High School; and Eric Nadelstern, principal, International High School, 13 June, 2001.

McMullan, Bernard J., Cynthia L. Sipe, and Wendy C. Wolf. *Charters and Student Achievement: Early Evidence from School Restructuring in Philadelphia.* Bala Cynwyd, PA: Center for Assessment and Policy Development, 1994.

McMullan, Bernard J. *Trends in Student Achievement among Students Enrolled in Philadelphia's Comprehensive High Schools 1988/89 to 1995/96.* An Update Prepared for The Pew Charitable Trusts.

Meier, Deborah. "Can the Odds Be Changed? What It Will Take to Make Small Schools Ordinary Practice." In *Creating New Schools: How Small Schools Are Changing American Education*, edited by Evans Clinchy, 183-190. New York: Teachers College Press, 2000.

Payne, Charles M., and Mariame Kaba. "So Much Reform, So Little Change: Building-Level Obstacles to Urban School Reform." Unpublished manuscript available at http://www.temple.edu/CPP/rfd/So_Much_Reform.pdf

Philadelphia Public School Notebook, spring 2000. "Federal Court to Hear Bias Case," 15.

Philadelphia Public School Notebook, spring 2000. "Philadelphia School Funding: Questions and Answers," 14.

Philadelphia Schools Collaborative. *Philadelphia Schools Collaborative. Narrative Final Report.* Philadelphia: Philadelphia Schools Collaborative, 1995.

Pittman, Robert B., and Perri Haughwout. "Influence of High School Size on Dropout Rate," *Educational Evaluation and Policy Analysis* 9, no. 4 (1987): 337-343.

Raywid, Mary Anne. *Taking Stock: The Movement to Create Mini-Schools, Schools-within-Schools, and Separate Small Schools.* Urban Diversity Series. New York: ERIC Clearinghouse on Urban Education, Teachers College, Columbia University, 1996.

Raywid, Mary Anne. *Focus Schools: A Genre to Consider.* Urban Diversity Series. New York: ERIC Clearinghouse on Urban Education, Teachers College, Columbia University, 1994.

Raywid, Mary Anne. "Mapping Progress toward Restructuring: One School's Story." Paper presented at the annual meeting of the American Educational Research Association, San Francisco, CA, April 1995.

Rizzo, Judith A. "School Reform: A System's Approach." In *Creating New Schools: How Small Schools Are Changing American Education*, edited by Evans Clinchy, 133-149. New York: Teachers College Press, 2000.

Russo, Alexander. "From Frontline Leader to Rearguard Action: The Chicago Annenberg Challenge." In *Can Philanthropy Fix Our Schools? Appraising Walter Annenberg's $500 Million Gift to Public Education*, 35-50. New York: Thomas B. Fordham Foundation, 2000.

Schipps, Dorothy, Joseph Kahne, and Mark A. Smylie. "The Politics of Urban School Reform: Legitimacy, City Growth, and School Improvement in Chicago." *Educational Policy* 13, no. 4 (1999): 518-545.

Small Schools Coalition, Business and Professional People for the Public Interest, and Leadership for Quality Education. *Small Schools: Hopeful Beginnings: An Initial Report on Chicago's RFP Small Schools.* Chicago: Small Schools Coalition, Business and Professional People for the Public Interest, and Leadership for Quality Education, 1999.

Smith, Gregory A. "Living with Oregon's Measure 5: The Costs of Property Tax Relief in Two Suburban Districts." *Phi Delta Kappan* 76, no. 6 (1995): 452-461. ERIC Document Reproduction Service No. EJ497518.

Smylie, Mark, Diane Bilcer, J. Kochanek, K. Sconzert, K. Shipps, and H. Swyers. *Getting Started: A First Look at Chicago Annenberg Schools and Networks.* Chicago: Annenberg Research Project, 1988.

Special Focus Schools Task Force. *Special Focus Schools: Providing Innovation and Choice in Public Education.* Portland, OR: Portland Public School District, 1999.

Spielman, Fran. "City High Schools May Get Smaller: Daley Says Proper Size Is 400 to 500 Students." *Chicago Sun-Times*, 8 June 1995, 6.

Stiefel, L., P. Latarola, N. Fruchter, and R. Berne. *The Effects of Size of Student Body on School Costs and Performance in New York City High Schools.* New York: Institute for Education and Social Policy, New York University, 1998.

Stockard, J., and M. Mayberry. *Effective Educational Environments.* Newbury Park, CA: Corwin Press, 1992.

Vallas, Paul. *Saving Public Schools*, Civic Bulletin no. 16. New York: Manhattan Institute, 1999. ERIC Document Reproduction Service No. ED446397.

Wasley, Patricia A., Michelle Fine, Matt Gladden, Nicole E. Holland, Sherry P. King, Esther Mosak, and Linda Powell. *Small Schools: Great Strides: A Study of New Small Schools in Chicago.* New York: The Bank Street College of Education, 2000. ERIC Document Reproduction Service No. ED465474.

Index